BREAKING THE ICE

To
Nella Dan,
'the little red ship',
her crew and the ANARE personnel
who sailed in her

BREAKING THE ICE

Rowan Butler

AN ALBATROSS BOOK

1943-G

Published in Australia and New Zealand by
Albatross Books Pty Ltd
PO Box 320, Sutherland
NSW 2232, Australia
in the United States of America by
Albatross Books
PO Box 131, Claremont
CA 91711, USA
and in the United Kingdom by
Lion Publishing
Icknield Way, Tring
Herts HP23 4LE, England

First edition 1988

National Library of Australia
Cataloguing-in-Publication data

Butler, Rowan
Breaking the Ice

ISBN 0 86760 087 X (Albatross)
ISBN 0 7459 1189 7 (Lion)

Bibliography
Includes index

1. Antarctic regions — Description and travel
I. Title

998'.9

Front cover photograph: A crevasse scene from the documentary film,
'Douglas Mawson — The Survivor'
Back cover photograph: Nella Dan in Horseshoe Harbour, Mawson,
Antarctica
Photographic credits:
All photographs were taken by the author except as noted below.
The following people assisted the author with the particular
photographs on the pages indicated: B. Baxter, photo of the
author; R. Kennedy, p.23; M. Haste, p.38 (top); J. Peiniger, p.56
(bottom); E. Szworak, p.86 (bottom); A. Wood, p.95 (top); J. van
Franeker, p.100 (centre).
Pictures by the author which are Antarctic Division official
photographs appear on the following pages: p.74 (bottom); p.88
(bottom); p.113 (top); p.120; p.129; p.131 (bottom); p.135
(bottom). Antarctic Division supplied the icecap cross-section
photograph on p.70. The bottom centre and bottom right pictures on
p.91 are Antarctic Division photographs by Qin Dahe.
Art Forms Australia Pty Ltd, who hold the copyright of the
photograph on p.34, kindly gave permission for its use.

Typeset by Rochester Communications, Sydney
Printed by Mandarin Offset, Hong Kong

Contents

Foreword

'IT'S FOR MEN who can take it!' was the tongue-in-cheek catchcry during my year at Davis, my presence having terminated the all-male wintering tradition at the Australian continental Antarctic stations.

This and much else had changed since the early expeditions. As a girl I used to visit Captain Morton Moyes who went to Antarctica with Mawson in 1911. His soul-stirring accounts of isolation, deprivation, snowblindness, adventure and scientific experiments against adversity fired my enthusiasm to go. While different in era and style from those now remote days, this book has its own drama and excitement and is as good an account of modern 'Antarctic man' as I have found anywhere.

A second valuable feature of the book is the care and accuracy evident in the scientific work that the author and other researchers undertake. There are problems in making and monitoring scientific equipment in such an environment. When things go wrong, the author shows how problems are worked on, not glossed over. Despite the financial and political constraints on scientists evident in Australia as much as elsewhere, it is an ideal laboratory for any boffin

studying human and animal behaviour, and any number of disciplines ranging from the study of lakes to geomagnetic micropulsations. It is still the expensive, apparently impractical theoretical studies which yield important results once analysed. The variation of atmospheric gases locked into each ice core sample and its implications for changing global climate is one example.

A third way in which this book is important is that it is a fitting tribute to the *Nella Dan* and her crew. The ship recently ran aground on Macquarie Island and was scuttled at sea in December 1987 when salvage was not feasible. The *Nella* and her crew have contributed significantly to Australia's post-war Antarctic program and many expeditioners, including Rowan, have fond memories of her.

In some respects the so-called heroic age in Antarctica is over: there are still, however, the challenges that experimental research, isolation and adversity place before people, challenges understood and taken up by the author. I commend this book by my good friend Rowan to you.

Louise Holliday
Sydney, Australia

Acknowledgements

TO THE PEOPLE who helped me in the writing of this book I wish to say a heartfelt thank you: Dr Paul White, who was the catalyst in the beginning and a wise adviser on many aspects; and John Waterhouse, publisher, and Ken Goodlet, editor, for their enthusiasm, encouragement and guidance from the start.

I appreciate the help given by those who read and offered comments and suggestions on the text, particularly Charles Lethbridge, David Byers, Knowles Kerry and Peter Gormly. I would also like to thank Arne Sørensen and many of the staff at Antarctic Division, in particular Des Lugg and Peter Keage, for answering questions as I checked facts.

The manuscript was ably typed by Marianne Kuilenburg and Henry Nugteren, who generously gave of their time, as did Bill Breeze, who assisted with the proofreading.

I am indebted to Bob Reeves for his nurturing of my photographic abilities by way of encouragement, advice and opportunities given for practical experience.

And thank you, God, for making such a splendid world for us to enjoy.

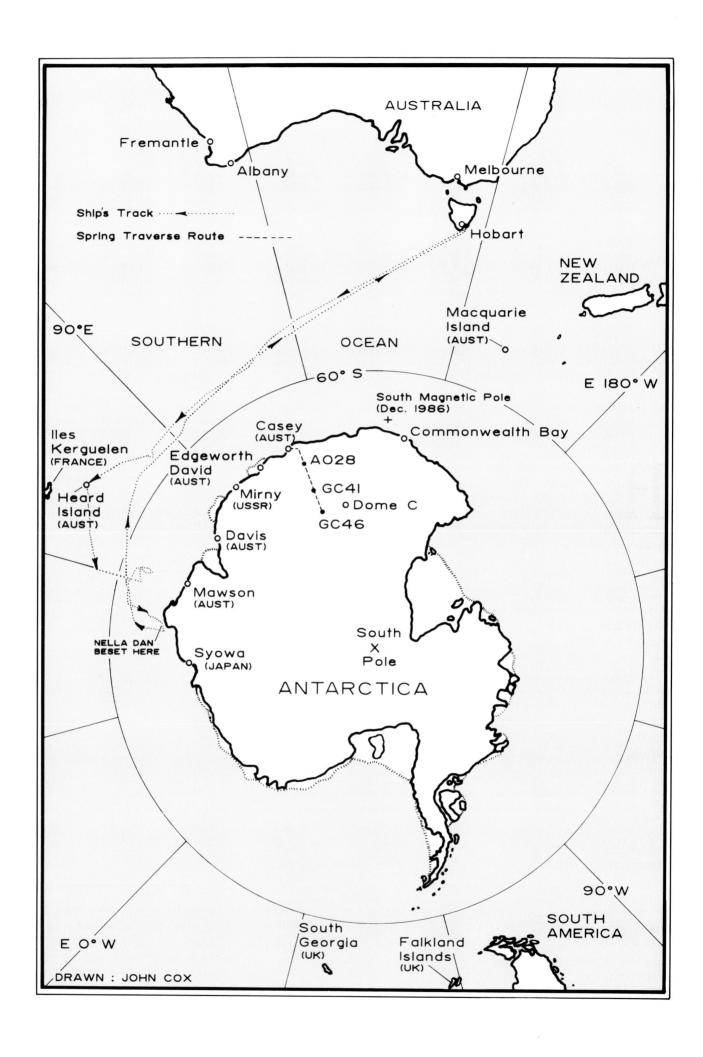

1
Heading south

'HAVE YOU GOT THE poles in place yet?' I yelled.

'They'll be right in a moment,' John shouted back through the noise and half-dark.

'Just keep a firm grip!' I continued to hang onto the chaotically flapping tent. Stinging snow, driven horizontally by galeforce wind, lashed our faces. Squinting through the mirk, I could see Paul had the other end of the tent secure. After a few more minutes' stumbling about, the three of us completed erecting our thin shelter, crawled through the tubular entrance sleeve and tied it off, sealing out the blizzard.

I was sharing the tent with John Peiniger, cosmic ray engineer, Paul Butler, Officer in Charge of Mawson, and one uncomfortable big rock under the middle of the floor. As dinner cooked over the primus stove, filling the air with steam and making everything damp, I reflected on our situation: here we were at Langford Gap in rough and cramped conditions, while a few kilometres away

people would be sitting around dining tables being served four-course meals and sweating from the heat of open fires and electric blankets in the ski lodges of Falls Creek in the Victorian Alps.

I enjoyed every minute of the week's field training though, and there was no way I would have swapped my position there and the prospect of a year in Antarctica for a place on the ski slopes. The three of us were part of a larger group that was training for the 1981 Australian National Antarctic Research Expeditions (ANARE). We were taught new skills and improved existing ones in the areas of crevasse rescue, abseiling, snow and ice work, cross-country skiing, orienteering and first aid.

Back in Melbourne, the training continued with a St John first aid course and a day at the Metropolitan Fire Brigade Training College with hot, smoky and wet lessons in extinguishing blazing buildings. Fire is one of the greatest hazards in Antarctica as it can swiftly destroy invaluable shelter and supplies and in the dry, windy

conditions it is difficult to put out. The Army took us out to Port Phillip Bay to become familiar with their amphibious vehicles called LARCs (Lighter: Amphibious Resupply Cargo) which are used to unload the relief ships at the Antarctic bases because there are no wharf facilities.

At the Royal Melbourne Hospital I learnt about anaesthetics. Two volunteers from each of the bases (Casey, Davis, Mawson and Macquarie Island) were taught how to work an anaesthetic machine and two others trained as surgeon's assistants — invaluable if an operation were necessary. Most of our tutoring was done in the operating theatres and, in a fascinating two weeks, we witnessed everything from brain surgery to the removal of ingrown toenails! Soon after, I had to go under the knife myself and give up my back teeth — four impacted wisdom teeth — before the dentist would give me a dental clearance certificate — one of the requirements before being allowed to go south.

After having seen others off on earlier ships, it was my turn to sail on 9 January 1981 for Mawson. At the wharf we were addressed by the then Secretary of the Department of Science and Technology, Dr John Farrands. The formalities over, the assembled expeditioners boarded *Nella Dan* and took up vantage points on the ship from which to wave farewell to well-wishers on the wharf. The excitement of leaving for Antarctica overcame any sadness I felt about not seeing my family and friends for over a year. A large blue and white banner held up on the wharf read

'Mawson Goodbye and Good Luck!' as streamers trailed in the water and we sailed down the Yarra River and out into Port Phillip Bay. The *Thala Dan*, on its return from the French Antarctic base of Dumont d'Urville, passed us as we headed out of the bay for the open waters of Bass Strait and the stormy Southern Ocean.

On my first morning at sea I missed most of breakfast due to oversleeping and only managed to grab a couple of slices of bread and vegemite. This was fortuitous. Within half-an-hour I was feeling decid-

Above: The farewell to *Nella Dan*'s passengers, Melbourne
Below: *Nella Dan* heads south

edly queezy and made it to my bunk in the nick of time. Clanging alarm bells roused me at 10.30 am and I clambered to the boat deck where everyone assembled for a compulsory lifeboat drill. Ruben Nielsen, the chief steward, lined us up according to our cabin numbers and demonstrated how to wear the life jackets.

'En, to, tre, fire . . .' he counted in Danish, ensuring everyone was there while the ship was checked for stowaways. I took quick glances at

those who had to break ranks
to feed the fish over the
varnished rail and was thankful
to be feeling reasonably well.
It was not long before most of
us found our sea legs and were
able to enjoy being up and
about.

Part of the voyage was to
be spent carrying out marine
science and oceanography
studies for the Australian contri-
bution to the First International
BIOMASS Experiment (FIBEX).
My time was divided between
helping in the final preparations
of the equipment for FIBEX,
reading, and watching the birds
following the ship. The black-
browed and wandering
albatrosses held my interest for
hours. Huge birds, the wan-
derers' wingspan being three to
four metres, they rarely flap
their wings, using the incessant
winds to carry themselves
along. My eyes followed one of
these living gliders: it soared
past the ship and circled astern;
slipped and vanished behind a
wave, smaller birds in train;
reappeared sweeping along the
face of the next dark, foaming
wall; and sliced the wavefront
with a Zorro-like slash of a
wingtip before rising high
above the reach of the wave's
leaping crest.

'Iceberg!' was the cry on
the morning of 14 January
which brought all the passengers running out on deck.
Cameras snapped away madly
and soon it became one of the
most photographed pieces of
ice in the Southern Ocean. The
'berg was many times longer
than the ship and the heights of
its brilliant, white sides stood
taller than *Nella*'s masts. The
ocean swell smoothed the base
of the rugged cliffs to rounded
contours and rebounded from
caves in explosions of spray.
This impressive sight made me
more eager than ever to reach
Antarctica.

Above: Antarctic marine fauna
Right: Wandering albatross

The iceberg was the first visible evidence of our southward progress. The temperature grew steadily colder, snow fell, there were more hours of daylight and finally we reached the pack ice — pieces of frozen ocean floating about. Although the pack with its birds and animals was a place of wonder and delight to the passengers, the ship tried to avoid it as far as possible. It slowed our progress markedly and, to my disappointment, we were in open water again before long.

Nella Dan was to call at Davis before going to Mawson and two days from our first landfall we rendezvoused with another ship, the *Nanok S*, which had just left Davis and was returning to Melbourne. Opportunities for sending mail to Australia from Antarctica are few and this one was not to be missed, so an arrangement was made to pass our mail over using a rope. *Nella*'s crew set up a rocket line and fired it across. The rope trailed neatly behind the missile as it flew over *Nanok* and then, to everyone's surprise and to some people's embarrassment, we saw the end of the line following as well. On attempt number two the end of the rope was securely tied. People stood back and the rocket hurtled between the vessels. Unfortunately, however, it left the line behind altogether! In the best tradition of 'the mail must go through', a third attempt was made. Those with red faces checked rocket and line more than once before it was suc-cessfully fired and our letters, sealed in multiple garbage bags, were hauled across the water. The exercise had been an interesting introduction to the 'Antarctic factor' which often brings catastrophe to the simplest of tasks. Thankfully we had not been trying to rescue a drowning man!

Three blasts on the ship's horn woke me at 5.15 am on the morning of 26 January. Stumbling out on deck to investigate, I discovered we had arrived at Davis. The sun shone brightly on surrounding icebergs and the rocky hills of the Antarctic mainland. I sleepily took in the picturesque view of this new shore before returning to the warmth of my bunk. It was the last time I saw the sun that day, for the sky became

overcast and it snowed, making it cold work for those unloading and ferrying cargo to shore on the LARCs. The following day the wind blew so strongly that unloading came to a halt, but the day after I planted my feet on the frozen continent.

The day was spent exploring the station and its surrounds both on foot and during a brief but revealing helicopter ride. From the chopper I could see the ice-free Vestfold Hills in which Davis is located, ending twenty-four kilometres to the east where they disappeared under a blanket of white stretching to the horizon. In the south, Crooked Fjord separated brown rock and the ragged edge of the Sørsdal Glacier from where many of the 'bergs which crowded the coastline had been calved.

On landing, I sought out a friend, the Davis Medical Officer Louise Holliday, who was about to become the first Australian woman to winter in Antarctica. We discussed the forthcoming year until it was time for me to return to *Nella Dan* and sail for Mawson.

After being delayed by bad weather, we approached Mawson on 3 February, sailing down 'Iceberg Alley'. This corridor lies over an underwater trench and is walled in by hundreds of icebergs grounded in the shallow water on either side. Behind the scattered islands which now lay ahead of us rose the Antarctic plateau, forming a flat horizon, but broken in places by jagged mountains thrusting from the ice sheet. *Nella Dan* stood off Mawson's Horseshoe Harbour waiting for our official welcome and I took in the view of the station — a group of buildings huddled on a tiny island of bare rock, jutting from the ice which pushed at its back door. It looked vulnerable to being swept down the slope into the sea by any fierce winds which blew off the mainland. Floating in the harbour was an iceberg which had been winched back from the entrance and was now tethered to the land.

Our greeting was an explosion on shore and, with this unusual 'ceremony' over, I stood at the bow of the ship, filled with anticipation and excitement as she slipped between the iceberg and the end of the protective peninsula called West Arm. Here a firmly guyed sign read 'It's Home, It's Mawson'.

After a few days ashore, Mawson did feel like home, but to house us satisfactorily for the year, it had to supply us with food, fuel and stores. Every item we might need came on the resupply ships — there were no supermarkets, fast food shops, barbers or television stations here. All the goods the ship carried had to be unloaded and everything came packed in wooden crates which required individual manhandling.

Above left: Elephant seals, Davis
Top: On *Nella Dan*'s bridge
Centre: *Nella Dan* at Mawson
Right: Passing a tabular iceberg

This was the same system Douglas Mawson had used for his 1911 expedition and it was thankfully the last season it was used by Antarctic Division. The following summer, boxes came packed in shipping containers, speeding up the unloading considerably.

Ferrying our provisions ashore continued until all outside work was stopped by a blizzard. I woke in the morning to find blinding clouds of dry, fallen snow, fine like talcum powder and called drift, being hurled along by the screaming wind. For a true blizzard, the wind must be thirty-four knots (63 km/h) or greater — in other words, galeforce — for one hour, the air laden with snow, visibility down to one hundred metres or less and the temperature below zero.

During this blow, the wind gusted at eighty-nine knots (165 km/h) and our so-called 'pet iceberg' in Horseshoe Harbour broke its leash, sealing off the entrance and trapping *Nella Dan*. The iceberg had originally floated in through a back way and became stuck when it

drifted to the entrance used by the ships. A heavy mooring line had been sent to Mawson earlier in the season for pulling it back out of the way. This was done from the shore and the 'berg was tied up, leaving room for a ship to come into the harbour. During the blizzard, the force of the wind blowing on the 'berg snapped the line.

When the weather abated the iceberg was dragged clear again, but a final solution came when the LARCs slowly pushed it out of the harbour the way it had first come in. It did not stay around long and by the following day had drifted out into Kista Strait and was heading westwards. In a surprise discovery later in the year, it was found during a dog trip far up the coast from Mawson, locked in the sea ice with the rope still around it.

The resupply was further delayed when one of the LARCs sank. While alongside *Nella Dan*, its load of steel pipes shifted, flipping the vehicle over. Although designed to be self-righting, the LARC was held

Above: Winching the sunken LARC to the surface

upside down by the weight of a crane mounted to it. Water entered through its deck and it went to the bottom within minutes. The LARC personnel were quickly rescued and later in the day a salvage attempt was made when a diver attached a line to the craft. It was hauled to the surface by the ship, pumped out by the other LARC and towed ashore. Later, after being overhauled in the vehicle workshop, it was put back into service.

Between the pace of unloading *Nella Dan* and later the *Nanok S*, there was normal work to be done and the old hands spent time with the newcomers showing them the ropes. Taking over from two others, I was to maintain and collect data from various experiments, mostly in the study of upper atmosphere physics. Colin McIntosh, a physicist, and Sjoerd Jongens, an electronics engineer like myself, described the running and idiosyncrasies of the experiments.

Above: A summer sunset at Mawson

'Up there in the ceiling is the all-sky camera,' Colin explained. 'It records auroras by taking horizon-to-horizon photographs every three minutes during the night.' A photometer for studying the temperature of the ionosphere, a receiver for recording very low frequency electromagnetic waves and clean air samplers were some of the other experiments in my care.

Ten of us who were to winter at Mawson would be doing scientific work. A cook, medical officer, carpenter, plumber, electricians, radio operators and technicians, diesel mechanics, officer in charge and building tradesmen — who were there for the station rebuilding program — brought the total to thirty-two.

We worked a six-day week, with Sunday off and Saturday afternoon for general duties around the station. There were rosters for 'slushy' (cook's helper for a week at a time) and nightwatch, where the assigned person made regular checks of

the buildings for fires, monitored the generators and completed other tasks.

One of the jobs was to clean the toilets in Law Hut. The toilet facilities were crude but effective: four two-hundred-litre drums were set in the concrete floor and had wooden seats fitted to them. The drums were partly filled with wood and briquettes and one of these was burnt off each night by the nightwatch. The wooden seat was removed, kerosene poured over the contents of the drum and a weighty steel lid with a ventilation hole placed over the top. The smoke escaped via a chimney on each drum.

On my first nightwatch there was no kerosene left and I was ignorant as to what the fuel actually was or where to get it, so I sought the advice of a more experienced expeditioner.

'You use ATK — that's aviation turbine kerosene which is used in the bulldozers,' he said. 'Make sure you take the right stuff. You know that jagged hole in the ceiling of Law Hut?'

'Yes,' I replied.

'Well, that was the result of someone using petrol instead of ATK. It blew that heavy lid straight up!' Enough said. I made certain of the correct fuel!

A sewage treatment plant now handles the waste from the new 'Red Shed' which houses the surgery and the expeditioners' modern bedrooms, called dongas. In 1981, the dongas were in prefabricated huts, seven to a hut, each room being about a bedlength square with a curtain across the doorway and containing a raised bunk with a built-in desk, drawers and hanging space. At one end of the huts was a shower and, although we were better off than in the days of bucket showers, a rule was made to have only two seven-minute showers a week because of the scarcity of water. The water was obtained by melting the icecap in a small man-made lake behind the station and pumping it into holding tanks. Despite having the majority of the world's fresh water in our back-yard, Antarctica's covering of ice and snow had first to be

melted, an expensive operation when fuel oil has to be bought and shipped from Australia to provide the heat.

The final ship of the season, *Nanok S*, sailed from Mawson on 13 March, taking the last of the previous year's winterers and those who had stayed for the summer. We were alone.

Being cut off from the rest of the world was one of the things I found attractive about Antarctica. I had come for the adventure and to see and experience a grand continent. The rush of city life I had been used to in Australia was not a

great loss to me. I liked the lifestyle of being catered for, being my own boss and having a view of ice cliffs, mountains and glaciers on the short walk to work. For me, being paid to work here seemed a bonus — although some people do go south for the money as it is an excellent opportunity to save. Some go to escape people or situations, to engage in soul-searching, or to return to a place previously enjoyed.

Whatever our personal reasons for being there, the real reason we were in Antarctica was political. Australia has for a long time been active in this

region and in 1933 the government of Great Britain transferred sovereignty of the area now called Australian Antarctic Territory to the Australian Commonwealth Government. This transfer was ratified by the Australian Government in 1936. Australia, wishing to demonstrate to the world a continuing interest in the area, maintains a presence by manning the three mainland bases of Mawson, Davis and Casey and undertakes valuable scientific work. Under the Antarctic Treaty, though, all land claims have been set aside and nations are free to build bases wherever they wish and

agree to share the results of their scientific endeavours.

One result of this sharing of scientific knowledge and the friendliness which exists under the Treaty was that we had a scientist from the USSR with us at Mawson. Eugene Poltev worked in the aeronomy building with four of us and we all became friends. To me, he was an ordinary person with the same hopes and fears as Australians.

Above: The Russians visit Mawson
Below: Eugene Poltev
Below right: Ron Kennedy with vegetables grown hydroponically

Eugene had spent the previous winter at Mawson and was due to be shipped out. On 1 May a helicopter flew in from the *Mikhail Somov* which was beyond the horizon. Sea ice had formed over the water, preventing the ship from getting closer. After the helicopter landed, Eugene and Paul Butler entertained the VIPs while the rest of us bartered with the other Russians for hats, mittens and badges. Although George Hedanek was the only one of us who could speak any Russian, we had a hearty time together. I found that friendships here were not interfered with by politics, which often ruins relations in other parts of the world.

The *Mikhail Somov* had come to Mawson via Melbourne and was able to bring us mail. When we waved goodbye to Eugene, the helicopter was also carrying mail from us to be sent home via diplomatic channels and the post. From then on our only means of contact with the outside world was by radio. The normal communication channels were radio telephone ('radphone') — where a sked was made twice daily to Sydney Radio, linking us with the Australian telephone network — and telex.

Two hundred free telex words a month were allowed for personal messages. To save on words, codes for standard phrases were used and the telexes themselves were usually referred to as 'WYSSAs' — the code for 'All my love darling'. I had a radio amateur's licence and, through my contact in Sydney, I was able to talk with my family once a week. Personal messages were also received on 'Calling Antarctica', a weekly Radio Australia program. Our 'newspaper' was a daily telex news bulletin which I only read occasionally. The important events of the world held little significance for me in my isolation.

All these connections could be broken though for days on end, leaving the station so solitary and beyond civilisation that it might well have been on another planet. This cut in communications occurred if there was a polar cap absorption (PCA), when the radio waves which were normally reflected back to earth travelled straight out into space because of the absence of the necessary reflecting layer in the ionosphere. The effect is related to sunspot activity and is more pronounced in the polar regions. During a PCA, the

radio operator had little to do, but the problem has now been overcome with the use of satellite communication systems as they are unaffected by PCAs.

I sent telexes to many of my friends as midwinter approached, asking them to the Mawson midwinter dinner. Many prominent and not so prominent people were invited by us and my most memorable invitation and reply was:

Mawson 05 Jun

To the Prince of Wales,
Buckingham Palace, London,
United Kingdom.
His Royal Highness, The Prince of Wales:

Your Highness, the Lady Diana and yourself are cordially invited to attend the midwinter dinner at Mawson, Antarctica on the twenty-first of June.

As you opened our new headquarters at Kingston, Hobart earlier this year, I thought you may like the opportunity to inspect Australia's premier Antarctic station. A trip to the Prince Charles Mountains can be arranged.

If you are unable to fly to the base, transport via dog sled can be arranged from the edge of the sea ice.

Yours faithfully,
Rowan Butler

Above and below: Midwinter dinner

Buckingham Palace London
17 Jun

Mr Rowan Butler
Australian National Antarctic
Research Headquarters
Kingston Hobart Tasmania

(Mawson)

The Prince of Wales and the Lady Diana Spencer have asked me to thank you for your kind invitation to attend the midwinter dinner at Mawson Antarctica on 21st June. I am afraid however that they are unable to accept since they have already made their plans for that day.

Francis Cornish
Assistant Private Secretary

None of our invited guests turned up in the end, so we made do with our own company.

Midwinter had gradually come upon us, heralded by lower temperatures and dwindling hours of daylight. The surface of the harbour began to freeze after mid-March and clusters of ice crystals called anchor-ice grew on the rocks under the water. Some of these broke free of the bottom and floated about, looking like small crystal chandeliers. Sea ice slowly formed a hard crust over the bays around Mawson and on the ocean to the horizon.

Mawson station in winter

This white shell was broken during a blizzard in April when it cracked up and drifted out to sea, driven along by the powerful wind. The ice added to the pack far to the north where the wildlife now fed, the animals and birds having deserted the coast to man.

The days faded like a sunset. The sun arched low in the sky for a couple of hours, then less, appearing as half a disc creeping across the horizon, intermittently hidden by icebergs, until it was finally extinguished by the tilt of the world. At noon during the two weeks we were completely without the sun, only a twilight glowed in the northern sky.

The restrictions and tensions brought about by the long hours of darkness were at least temporarily dispelled by celebrating midwinter and at Antarctic stations this is the social event of the year. We celebrated in the traditional manner with a sumptuous dinner — prepared by our cook, Allan Winter — and a performance of a somewhat rewritten version of 'Cinderella'. Also on the agenda was the Horseshoe Harbour Derby held midmorning out on the ice. The moon shone down from a clear, starry sky and a cold wind blew drift about us as we gathered for the start. Runners, a skier towed by a skidoo, a manned wheelbarrow and vehicles of various kinds sped around the dark harbour in the madcap event. A farm tractor fitted with halftracks appeared out of the gloom, clattered over the line and won.

In the days following the midwinter festivities, we looked forward to the dawning of another season of light.

Top left: Mawson coastline in winter, David Range in background
Top: The Cinderella play
Centre: The start of the
Horseshoe Harbour Derby
Right: Aurora australis

2
Slots and sledging

T HERE WAS NEVER A
shortage of work to
do at Mawson, but spare
time could be filled in a
variety of ways. We relaxed in
the recreation room which held
a library, records, tapes and a
billiard table or there were
films and videos to watch.
Celebration parties were held
— for any reason — or special
events organised, such as a
dress-up evening or playing
Davis in a darts competition

over the radio. Some people
pursued hobbies, there being a
good stock of materials available and, with the diversity of
jobs on the station, we had the
opportunity to learn new skills
from one another. Photography
became popular with everyone
and a lot of time was spent in
the darkroom developing and
printing pictures. Around the
station we could go walking, go
'bumsliding' down snow drifts
under the icecliffs on plastic

sheets, or sail homemade ice
yachts on the frozen sea.

When feeling cooped up
by being restricted to the
Mawson locale, it was possible
to organise much-looked-
forward-to field trips, referred
to as jollies. The first I went on
after midwinter was by skidoo
to the Auster emperor penguin
rookery and I did not realise
how much I wanted to get
away until I had the opportunity.

Late in the morning of 30 June, with a few stars still twinkling above, Derry Craig, Don Dettman, Wally Elliot and I set out eastwards down the coast. The flush of dawn in the north turned the vast sea ice plain, the coastal ice cliffs and the clear sky pastel shades of pink and blue.

'What was the temperature when we left?' I asked Don as I tucked in behind him on the back of the skidoo, trying to keep out of the wind.

'About minus fifteen or twenty,' he replied. 'We'll stop soon and warm up.'

Sitting still on the skidoos while zipping over the icy highway was a cold business despite wearing down jackets and lots of woollies, so we halted and danced around, waving arms and beating mitts together. On our way again, the sun gradually peeped over the horizon and for forty-five minutes slid along the bottom of the sky, providing light but not heat.

Reaching Macey Island, we unloaded our gear from the sleds and carried it to the hut. After the radio antenna was set up, I sat on top of the island in the waning dusk. Behind me in the distance the flat sea ice ended abruptly in the vertical ice cliffs of the mainland, while to my right lay a myriad of icebergs.

Auster emperor penguin rookery

These 'bergs were grounded on the shallow sea floor, effectively anchoring the surrounding sea ice and preventing it from breaking out during a blizzard. It is on such safe areas of fast ice that emperor penguins choose to establish their rookeries because they breed during winter on the sea ice. We would search amongst the icebergs for the birds the next day.

For now, I looked northwards where, in the overall stillness, local winds suddenly gusted powerfully, first from one direction then another. Without rationality they blew from all points of the compass, starting and stopping as though being turned on and off. Great clouds of drift swept up from the ice, swirled about icebergs and spiralled into the air. With a sudden rushing noise I was hit by a fierce squall which blew over my camera mounted on its tripod and I lunged desperately, barely catching it centimetres from the ground. Moments later, all was calm again and, after gazing at this bizarre scene a little longer, the

stars shining overhead, I sought the warmth and protection of the hut.

After it grew light enough the following morning, we started off and were soon travelling down a long corridor between icebergs. At a stop, Derry noticed a distant thin, black line which we rightly guessed was the penguins, thousands of them grouped together for mutual warmth. We parked the skidoos and, as we walked towards the rookery, the birds turned to watch, some of them filing out to meet us. Most stood around, covering and warming with a fold of their lower breast a single egg which rested on their feet. When they moved about, the best they could manage was a slow shuffle.

These birds incubating the eggs were the males and they had taken on the two-month-long job after the eggs had been laid. At that time the female goes off to fatten up amongst the pack ice and returns later to take over feeding the newly-hatched chick.

The males go without food from the time the penguins gather at the rookery, one to two months before the female lays, until the chick has hatched. In poor condition, father walks perhaps fifteen kilometres or more over the frozen ocean to feed. The parents then share this cycle, though the ice edge usually gets closer to the rookery as summer nears.

Here, in quiet dignity, stood a community to be marvelled at, weathering blizzards in tightly packed huddles, patiently cradling and protecting the fragile new life balanced on their feet. Some emperors without responsibilities drew within a metre of me and examined their visitor or bent over to inspect my camera bag. The most aggressive went through a passive display of bowing and uttering a call to ward off the intruder. Others stretched their necks above their fellows to see what was going on, showing a beautiful sheen on their white and gold feathers even in the softness of the indirect light.

Bordering the rookery on one side was a long cliff of ice, wrought through with cracks and holes, towering into the sky. Blocks of fallen ice littered the mysterious canyons between surrounding 'bergs. The shadowed sides of blue, white and grey of these frozen monoliths supported sunlit peaks of pink, while a delicately-hued sky vaulted above it all. I later reflected in my diary in these words:

Being at the rookery and amongst the icebergs was incredible, like nothing I have ever experienced; so fascinating and weird that I could have been in a different world after having conjured it up in my imagination. The feeling of immensity, strangeness and beauty could never be captured in a photograph. The place is equal but different to any I have ever seen.

For me this was foreign beauty; for there were no trees, flowers, violent splashes of colour, mountains or lakes to enhance the landscape, no tremendous noise to overwhelm me: the scene was subtle, soft in colour, sound and mood — yet majestically grand. Here was a world within a world, an exquisite gem in the variety and extravagance of God's creation.

On our way back to the hut and on the following day while returning to Mawson, we set up bamboo canes along the route so other parties could navigate easily. Canes are light and strong and have been used as markers since the early days of Antarctic exploration. In crevassed areas it is wise to stick closely to the marked track as some of us were yet to discover for ourselves.

In August, seven of us left Mawson for a three-day break and to take some sleds of fuel drums inland where they would be picked up later on another trip. The transport this time was three bulldozers towing living vans, generator vans and fuel sleds. These are called tractor trains and any trip of reasonable length is referred to as a traverse.

Travelling up the slopes from the coast, we noticed the ice was bare of snow cover and we crossed the occasional small crevasse. The crevasses, commonly called slots, were no more than half a metre wide and, with snow filling the opening, were easy to see against the blue ice. In vehicles, these presented no problems unless a sled runner was parallel with a crevasse and fell in.

Above: Auster emperor penguin rookery in July
Left: Emperor penguins in summer

In mildly crevassed areas, slots are usually choked with snow near the surface or are spanned by a snow bridge which may be icy and hard and of varying thickness. The bridges are impossible to identify, though, if the ground is snow-covered. Crevasses form when an obstacle such as a mountain or a buried hill of rock impedes the flow of the slowly moving ice which cracks as it is distorted.

The bulldozers trundled south between the Masson and David Ranges and we left the exposed ice behind. The canes showed the track making a dogleg to the right towards Mt Elliot, but we started to cut straight across to Hordern Gap as George Hedanek, who was in charge, had been taken this way during the summer by some of the 1980 crew. Half a kilometre later, Don Dettman's voice came over the radio: 'I've opened up a slot, George.'

These still being novel to us, we stopped and stood around the metre-wide hole. Don's bulldozer tracks in the snow were half missing where part of the lid of the crevasse had fallen in.

'I wouldn't like to have stepped on that,' I said, peering down into the nothingness.

'That's for sure!' replied George. 'We'd better check ahead to see if there are any more. Use the bars on the 'dozer blades.'

These pointed, two-metre steel poles carried on the bulldozers were to test for crevasses. Peter (Jock) McLennan and I roped up and smashed at the surface with the bars, while the others used ice axes. Fifteen metres ahead of where George's leading vehicle had stopped, we found another crevasse two to three metres wide, wide enough for a tractor to break through and become stuck in the top. A 'dozer dropping unannounced into a slot comes as quite a shock to the

Above: The fallen sleds
Right: Jock digs for fuel drums

driver and, after he hopefully has the presence of mind to turn off the machine, he generally makes a lightning exit through the roof hatch and may then require a change of underwear!

Faced with this airy moat, we felt the obvious course was to make a smart about-turn and get back on the marked track. We checked the ground where the 'dozers would have to turn. Despite being roped up, I felt unnerved when poling the surface if the bar slipped freely through and I knew I was standing on a hidden chasm. Would the snow bridge hold or

not? One foot suddenly dropping through to the ankle had me trying to levitate as I ballet-leapt for safe ground. The surface had held, otherwise I would have disappeared as if through a trapdoor before being able to prevent it.

No significant slots were found and George started back, towing three fuel sleds. He told us later he felt one side of the bulldozer break through the surface. This was the opening of a dramatic incident for us which I recorded at the time in the following words:

All of us were standing well back and watching when I noticed the first fuel sled dip into what I realised was a hole in a now-broken snow bridge. The sled got across and the second moved over the gap, tipped up and silently vanished! We stared incredulously. I thought, 'Oh well, that's that, the third sled will probably stop on the edge.' George had pulled up and, with our eyes transfixed, the last sled slid slowly towards the hole, tilted and disappeared. We stood dumbfounded! The hole was not visible from where we were and the sleds had seemed to vanish into the ground without a sound.

Racing across to the hole, we found a tangled mess of sleds and fuel drums in a four-metre-wide crevasse. At this spot the crevasse had been blocked with snow about seven metres down, stopping the drums falling into the depths. The two sleds were still attached via their towing cables to the first on the surface. There was little which could be done in the remaining daylight, so we left everything where it was. Ropes were strung between the living vans that night as safety lines. The area was a minefield of varying-sized slots and we did not relish the idea of the earth

swallowing us up.

All the trains were now on the wrong side of 'George's slot' and, although they had crossed it safely on the way out, we spent the following day winching them back across one at a time. George and Don, being responsible for the vehicles, were much happier men after this was accomplished. A sixty knot (111 km/h) wind blowing a thick blanket of drift to the height of the vans kept us inside the next day, despite the sun shining brightly above it all.

The third day after the sleds had been 'slotted' we began work to extricate them and the forty-eight drums of fuel. The sight in the hole was now very different — blowing drift of the previous day had buried everything. Jock and I descended into the maw, attached to fixed ropes in case the floor fell out from underneath us. Digging down to the uppermost sled, we attached a steel cable from a bulldozer winch but, when the winch was started, the 'dozer was pulled back towards the hole while the sled remained firmly embedded in the snow. With the help of Peter Jacob and Ross McShane digging, enough snow was cleared to allow both sleds to be winched to the surface.

Day four was spent mining for fuel drums in the mound of drift. During the afternoon shift, Peter, Jock and I dug while George, Don, Ross and Heinz Dittloff hoisted the drums to the surface and loaded them onto a sled. I preferred working down the hole out of the wind, especially under the protection of the snow bridge which was very sturdy in that section. Drift continued to pour into the hole, making the figures working above misty silhouettes while they looked down onto the eddying white powder.

The drift kept filling the hole, but fortunately we could shovel it faster. It was thrown back under the lid of the crevasse and over the edge of our suspended snow floor which dropped off into bluey-black oblivion.

Having recovered almost half the drums, we made our exit from the area the next day, but not the way we had entered. Another large slot lay across our path, so we cautiously drove parallel with it and at last reached the track. Looked at objectively, the incident had been dangerous, but I found it an exciting experience and thought the inside of the crevasse a fascinating place.

Manhauling a sled is a far less comfortable way of journeying than travelling in a tractor train, but I did try it for one short trip. Puffing and straining as I pulled the large wooden sled along with three others, I concluded that Scott must have been crazy to have done this over vast distances and up a huge glacier to the South Pole. I was having problems on flat sea ice! If the means of getting about is to be traditional, I prefer dog sleds, the method in fact used by Amundsen who reached the

Above: Manhauling

South Pole ahead of Scott. In Antarctica, dogs have largely been replaced by vehicles, but are still recognised as being the safest means of transport over sea ice.

The dogs at Mawson were huskies and, though some were favourites, they were working animals rather than pets. I was surprised to find that they were not kennelled, but chained in lines on the snow. They are used to this and, being hardy, can cope with the cold conditions. In a blizzard they curl up with their backs to the wind and allow themselves to be drifted in, the snow acting as an insulator. To make sure they do not get completely buried they must be checked regularly. On one such occasion, I was helping dig out the long chain to which they were tethered so it could be brought to the surface. Finding a leash going off into the snow drift and thinking it was spare, I tried to pull it out. It was stuck fast and digging further revealed a dog's nose! He was more than half a metre under and the snow around him had frozen into an icy cast which was slowly suffocating him. With careful digging, Mark Haste and I were

able to heave him out and, although very weak, a night under cover restored him to health.

Though friendly and affectionate towards people, the dogs are jealous of each other and it is not wise to give a particular animal too much attention as the others will pick on it at the first opportunity. There is a pecking order in the canine community, largely determined by fighting prowess. The opportunity for a skirmish comes during trips and particularly at the start when they are taken across to the sled and attached to the rope traces. Someone must remain at the sled to keep order and, although dogs are put with others they are known to work well with, in their excitement of going for a run there is inevitably a brawl of some sort before leaving.

Working with the dogs gave me satisfaction and was fun despite the frustrations from a means of travel that has more than one mind of its own. They can also provide some lighter moments. On one occasion when I was farewelling a trip, an unsuspecting electrician got his ankle caught in a trace when the sled started off. He was dragged along on his back

until the driver, frantically shouting, 'Whoa boys! Whoa! Whoa!' while simultaneously applying all his weight to the brake, managed to stop the speeding sled. The impromptu stuntman was none the worse for wear and we all had a good laugh.

On the restart I was taking photographs from ahead. The dogs rushed towards me, so I stepped behind the 'cover' of a bamboo pole, thinking 'the dogs will go around it'. Dogs are not that smart. I ended in a heap with the broken cane, surrounded by a crowd of happy huskies. When they left for the

Above: Leaving Mawson by dogsled
Below: Steve Musgrove (left) and Bob Yeoman (right)

third time, I took photos from behind.

The longest dog trip of the year was undertaken by Paul Butler, John Gough, Jock McLennan and Bob Yeoman who travelled to Kloa emperor penguin rookery west of Mawson, covering over 530 kilometres between 23 September and 12 October. All my dog trips were within easy reach of Mawson and the first, in April, was to a hut at Rumdoodle in the Masson Range.

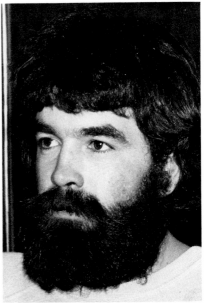

'Are you right to go?' Steve Musgrove called in carefully chosen words to the three at the other sled.

'We're set,' came the reply.

'Ready boys. . . mush!'

To have asked 'Are you ready?' could have led to a premature and rapid departure without us as the dogs knew that 'mush' — the signal to move — followed the 'ready' command and they were always impatient and eager to start.

There was more than one case of an escaping sled, like the time a team bolted after the driver had stopped and was tying his bootlace!

We rode on the sled initially because the dogs are full of enthusiasm and energy and race away. They soon slowed, ascending the ice slopes to the plateau and, as we trotted along at a steady pace, they scooped up mouthfuls of snow for a drink.

Above: Easy travelling over sea ice

Running or skiing alongside the sledge is the norm and the dogs recognise when you are being lazy by riding and will slacken their efforts, too. Some individuals learn the art of keeping their traces looking taut and act as if they are straining, but put no effort into pulling. If this is detected by either man or dog, they get a hard time.

At a stop along the way, I was the target of what seemed to be a dog's sense of humour. There are no trees in Antarctica. In a few moments of distraction, gazing at the horizon, I became another victim and the culprit was innocently sitting on the snow when I looked down and discovered my plight.

Arriving at our destination, the first task was to picket the dogs and attend to their needs, then we were free to set up camp and explore. Perched on a ridge of boulders and rock debris deposited by the moving ice plateau was the box-like orange hut. It was too cramped

with six in it, so Steve and I spent the night in a tent. To keep warm in the −20 °C temperature, we used two sleeping-bags and in the morning the only thing which could coax us out of them was hot porridge brought by Peter Longden.

In the afternoon Peter, Stuart Wolfe, John Gough and I walked around the base of part of the range and, climbing a scree slope, came upon Lake Lorna lying between the peaks of Fearn Hill and Mt Ward. We walked onto the lake, the thirty centimetre thick ice easily supporting our weight.

'It's like standing on a glass table,' Peter remarked as we looked through the transparent pavement at the rocks three metres below us. Cracks like white silk veils criss-crossed the ice, enhancing its beauty. Leaving this, we continued climbing onto the range and were rewarded with panoramic views of the mountains, the snowy plateau and the iceberg-dotted ocean basking under a brilliant sun.

Left and right: Husky pups at sleep and play

The most memorable time for me, though, on this jolly had come on the first day when we had time to investigate our surroundings. I had walked off and sat on a rock on the ice. In the distance, the hut was miniscule at the foot of the mountains and all living things were out of sight. The great ice sheet came from the far reaches of the inland past me, its rippled blue surface rolling down to the sea which carried on,

stretching white till held back by a thin band of fluffy cloud that let the limitless sapphire sky begin.

As I stared at the broken coastal ice cliff vanishing in the west, the silence was profound, the only sound an occasional twanging snap as the ice split. I felt very small, insignificant. Yet, though dwarfed by awesome surroundings, I knew I had real worth in the eyes of my loving Creator.

3
History on film

'PETER, HOW SHOULD I go about operating on Brian?' asked Paul Butler over the radio. The doctor, Peter Longden, was away from Mawson on a field trip so would not be there to do it himself.

'Don't worry about hygiene,' came the reply, 'just do it in the cold porch.' The radio operator at Davis who heard the conversation could

not believe his ears! The story quickly spread and Davis expeditioners felt glad they were not at Mawson. What they did not know at the time was that Brian was a dog. The minor operation was successful and so were the two carried out on humans that year — done in the small operating theatre. A broken nose was set and a skin graft operation performed and I was able to use my 'skills' as an anaesthetist.

The three graves on West Arm at Mawson testify to there being a limit to the resources of a doctor and a well-equipped surgery and operating theatre. Situations arise where particular treatment or equipment is required which is not available at the base. Specialist operations have been performed with instructions being given over the radio by experts in Australia, but sometimes evacuation of the patient is required and

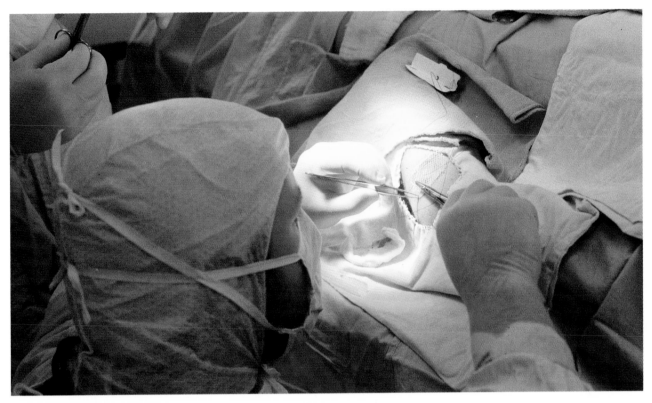

this is generally impossible. Three notable evacuations have taken place with the assistance and international cooperation that is characteristic of those working in Antarctica. American, New Zealand and Russian aircraft have all played parts in transporting two men from Davis to New Zealand — Col Perger in 1978 and Steve Bunning (who unfortunately died on the first leg of the journey) in 1985. In 1987, Vicki Aitken was flown from Mawson in a Russian helicopter and was transferred via two of their ships to Mauritius from where she was taken to Australia by air. Australia currently relies on ships to transport cargo and personnel to and from Antarctica and these only operate during the summer season.

The arrival of our first relief ship came more to my mind in early October after John Peiniger saw a skua fly around the base. While 'one skua does not a summer make', its presence was an indication that warmer weather was on the way. Soon the Adelie penguins would be marching across the ice to begin breeding on the islands around about, while snow petrels and Wilson's storm petrels would arrive to nest in crevices and under rocks.

Below left: Snow petrels nesting
Below: John Peiniger

The long winter nights had already been left behind and I was enjoying the fifteen hours of sunshine between sunrise and sunset. By the end of November there would be continuous daylight.

The light put an end to watching the auroras which had often produced an enchanting display in the night skies. More than once I had stood willingly in the bitter cold, my eyes fixed on a scene of delicate luminescence. Pale green vertical lines of light massed to create glowing curtains floating in a black velvet sky, the folds rippling and flowing in waves of movement as if shaken by an invisible hand. Perhaps their skirts were touched with lilac or their form was completely different — a starburst overhead or long, cloudlike streamers of light trailing across the star-spattered heavens. These noctilucent scenes would now be masked by perpetual light, but the Antarctic summer promised settings and events of its own, the most immediate being the arrival of helicopters from *Nella Dan*.

The sea ice at this time of year prevents the ships coming into the bases, so they tie up at the edge of the ice and helicopters fly in personnel and a limited amount of cargo. In the afternoon of 25 November I stood with an excited crew around the Mawson helipads. We welcomed three helicopters from *Nella* which were carrying the mail we were so eager for. Fresh fruit and vegetables were brought, too, and before they had reached the mess I had sampled a delicious orange. The mail was sorted on the billiard table by the designated postmaster, Ross McShane, who had plenty of help, and the letters and parcels were distributed.

Above: An aurora over the Masson Range
Left: The first mail for months
Above right: Traverse train, Hordern Gap

We crowded the recreation room, enthusiastically tearing open parcels and laughing at the contents of letters. Andrew Murray was pleased with his dozen bottles of much-loved HP sauce and most of us received items we missed or were short of. Necessities for the base were also flown in over the next two days — like the one hundred drinking mugs we had ordered from head office. When the box was opened, those of us looking on marvelled at the workings of a bureaucracy. We were now the proud possessors of one hundred saucers minus the matching cups!

Six of our number left on *Nella Dan*, but the influx of summer personnel began, mostly builders who worked hard erecting the new station buildings. The tank house for water storage was begun that summer and was erected close to the building I worked in, Aeronomy. Rock had to be blasted before they started and the first time this was done I stood on the roof of Aeronomy with Stuart Wolfe to watch and photograph the action.

'What will happen?' I asked Stuart, looking at the heavy rope blasting mats piled on the rock.

'Oh, the mats will probably lift about a metre when it goes off,' he answered. A bit boring, I think; no point in turning the camera sideways for a vertical shot. The fuse is lit and I stand waiting for the blast. Ka-who-o-o-m! A monstrous explosion of noise shakes me despite my having tried to steel myself for the moment, and the photo is snapped with an involuntary twitch of my fingers. I glance into the sky to see the mats being hurled upwards like sheets of paper and the air is full of fist-sized rocks thirty metres up and heading my way. Being on the roof I have nowhere to run and the only

course of action is to kneel down with my hands covering my head before the rocky shower clatters about us.

Stuart took it all a lot more calmly than I did, but it was fortunate that neither the two of us nor the three perspex domes and a delicate piece of equipment on the roof were hit. Some rocks punctured the metal skin of the roof and one mat landed next to Aeronomy, forty-five metres from the blast site. Those who had set off the eruption were as surprised as I was with the result. 'Still experimenting with the charge,' they explained.

A week later, I escaped the dangers of station life and left on a traverse to deploy an automatic weather station (AWS). This was another of the experiments for which I was responsible. The AWS consisted of a mast with various instruments on it which measured snow and air temperature, wind speed and direction, barometric pressure and the amount of incoming sunshine. This information, transmitted at regular intervals, was picked up by satellites and

relayed via them and an earth station to a computer in Toulouse, France. There it was stored and sent each month to the Antarctic Division's glaciology section. The AWS had been set up at Mawson the previous summer and during the year had suffered broken anemometer cups and the instrument mast snapping in two in strong wind.

The AWS was to gather information inland on the Antarctic plateau, and 12 December saw Derry Craig, Graham Dadswell, George Hedanek, Alan Marks, Mark Meyer, Allan Winter, Stuart Wolfe and myself heading off between the ranges in three tractor trains. In the next couple of days we lost sight of the mountains as we made our way south. Progress was slowed by difficulty in finding near-buried cane markers and by white-out conditions where the shadowless ground and overcast sky merged in grey oneness. I spent some of the travelling time skiing alongside the vehicles or getting a tow from a trailing rope.

The surface was smooth and free of sastrugi, the sometimes fantastically wind-scoured snow shapes which can reach two metres in height. Drift blowing over the surface sandblasts it into graceful carvings, often slender and undercut. Although beautiful, it may be a hindrance to travellers if large and hard — even to those driving bulldozers.

At the significant junction of 'Turners Turnoff', we found a lone sign in an endless white expanse pointing the way back to Mawson, straight on to Mt Creswell and right to Enderby Land. After looking both ways we turned right. Forty kilometres to the west we reached our destination and on 18 December the AWS was erected and switched on. I was able to test that the transmitter was functioning, but not whether the data being sent to the satellite system was correct. To check this it was necessary to radio Mawson and have someone there contact the appropriate people in Australia

Left: Alan Marks and George Hedanek

Above: Assembling the battery box

who in turn telexed France, obtained the latest figures and sent them back to me. Having to use this circuitous, slow but highly sophisticated route did seem a little ironic to me considering I was standing next to the transmit antenna! The communication loop occasionally broke down, too, due to public holidays in Australia.

The initial information showed the AWS was not working properly and this was confirmed on Christmas Eve. The next week was spent studying circuits, waiting out a blizzard, testing the instruments and celebrating Christmas and New Year. Christmas Day produced some T-shirt weather with the sun shining and no wind, so we made the most of it by kicking a football and throwing a frisbee around. When a breeze came up, though, it was too cold to go without a jumper, the temperature being −15 °C.

We had a Christmas tree, thanks to the ingenuity of George and Derry who made

The weather station at 'night' in summer

Above: Graham Dadswell abseiling.
A day off on the way home

covered the fault and that night was spent constructing a makeshift heater around the crystal, using resistors and polystyrene foam encased in an empty film container. The electronics box was buried again the next day and, after waiting overnight, I received a telex with good results, so we left for Mawson.

Four days after getting back, *Nanok S* arrived but was unable to reach the harbour as planned because the sea ice had not broken out. Three days were spent flying in as much cargo as possible and more new people, including the first woman any of us winterers had seen for ten months. Julie Campbell had come as the 1982 medical officer. We were also visited by some expeditioners from Davis who were returning home on *Nanok*, among them Louise Holliday. Her year in Antarctica had been enjoyable and worthwhile she said, despite a lack of acceptance by some of the men on her arrival at Davis. *Nanok* sailed on 15 January and, by the time the next ship reached us nine days later, *Nella Dan* again, the sea ice had broken out and she was able to moor in Horseshoe Harbour.

Two of the people who arrived on *Nella* this time were a husband-and-wife film team from the Australian Broadcasting Commission. David (Dave) Parer and Elizabeth (Liz) Parer-Cook had come to film a reconstruction sequence for a documentary about Australia's eminent Antarctic pioneer, Sir Douglas Mawson. The film was to be called 'Douglas Mawson — The Survivor'. The previous October I had been asked if I would play one of the three parts in the film and had readily agreed.

The reconstruction sequence was of the tragic dog sledge journey undertaken by Douglas Mawson, Xavier Mertz and Belgrave Ninnis in 1912.

one from a steel pipe with welding rods for branches. It was decorated with aluminium tags, sweets, streamers, tinsel, empty bottles and a star on top cut from a tin can. Presents from home stirred memories of loved ones back in Australia. I imagined friends lying on hot, sunny beaches as I stared through the window at a landscape where the same sun lit up a fuzzy tide of ground-drift which snaked its way over the frozen surface.

On New Year's Day we dug up the box containing the AWS electronics and I began to examine the circuitry. After repairing a minor problem and checking everything I could think of, I reconnected the box two days later. It was then I realised that the fault might be due to the cold and, as the testing had been done in the warmth of the van, I retrieved the electronics and rechecked it outside on the snow. It still operated correctly in the $-12\,°C$ temperature, so I cooled the vital components even further with a can of spray freeze. When a crystal oscillator suddenly jumped in frequency, I was sure I had dis-

They had left the Australasian Antarctic Expedition's (AAE) base at Commonwealth Bay and were 508 kilometres to the east before their progress came to a horrifying halt when Ninnis, the best of the two dog teams, most of the food, the tent, plus other vital pieces of gear were lost when they dropped through the lid of a crevasse. During the desperate slog back, the dogs were killed when they became too weak to pull and were used as food for the other dogs and the two men. Mawson's and Mertz's health deteriorated rapidly — their skin peeled off in sheets, their hair fell out and they suffered abdominal pains, diarrhoea, muscle and joint pain as well as cold and hunger. All the dogs perished and Mertz finally died in his sleep after becoming delirious and going through several fits. Eating the livers of the huskies, which contained very large amounts of vitamin A, poisoned the men's bodies and was the chief cause of their symptoms and Mertz's death.

Mawson then carried on alone after cutting the sled in half and throwing away every non-essential item to save weight. The situation seemed utterly hopeless and now his only aim was to get as close as possible to Commonwealth Bay so that his meticulous scientific observations and the record of the journey might be found by searchers. In his persistent march he survived falling into numerous crevasses. The first time was a particularly terrifying ordeal and he barely managed to climb back up the harness rope which he had knotted at intervals in case of such an emergency. After this, Mawson constructed a rope ladder which he strung between the sled and himself.

Above: David Parer films from a towed sled
Right: David Parer
Far right: Elizabeth Parer-Cook

Opposite, above and right: Scenes from the film 'Douglas Mawson — The Survivor'

Three weeks after Mertz had died, Mawson was still dragging the sled. Starving, and wondering how much longer the one kilogram of remaining food could be eked out, he discovered a snow cairn which he believed 'Providence' had guided him to. It held a precious cache of food and a note indicating it had been built that morning by a search party which had then turned back. With renewed determination he battled on and, after being delayed by a ferocious blizzard, reached the base ten days later to see the relief ship sailing away. Six men had been left at Commonwealth Bay in case the three overdue explorers returned and they attended to Mawson and radioed the ship. The *Aurora* came back, but was prevented from reaching the shore by strong gales. It left to pick up the expedition's Western Base party and the seven men had to wait another year before being taken back to Australia.

For me, to be involved in a film about this significant piece of Antarctic and Australian history was a privilege. I was to play the part of Mertz; Paul Butler, Mawson; and John Peiniger, Ninnis. I had read the story of their dreadful journey with particular interest in Xavier Mertz and tried to imagine the excitement, determination, grief, fear, despair and physical agony he had felt during the progress of the trip which ended for him in death.

In preparation for the filming, Dave and Liz spent their first week arranging many of the props with help from some of the expeditioners. The three 'actors' tried on their costumes and our maintenance carpenter, Ron Kennedy, doubled as hair stylist and gave me a suitable haircut. Helpers dug a hole in the ice a few kilometres from Mawson to simulate Aladdin's Cave, a shelter excavated by members of the AAE inland from Commonwealth Bay and used as a staging camp for their various sledging journeys. We were filmed at 'Aladdin's Cave' and on the ice behind Mawson between our normal work and as the weather permitted.

In early February, the entire complement of actors, producer, director, cameraman, sound recordist, makeup artist, grip and mechanic — all six of us — set up camp in traverse vans behind Mt Henderson, fifteen kilometres from Mawson. Three days were spent taking shots of camp scenes and travelling with the dogs. I skied in front of the sleds on a pair of old wooden skis which had been used on the AAE. They felt like large, heavy planks compared with my modern cross-country skis, but were more stable over the rough, rock-hard snow surface. This quickly stripped the tar and wax base from their undersides and they slipped about amongst the sastrugi. Mertz had been a champion skier, but it took all my concentration to remain upright in the tricky conditions.

On the fourth day, we went to film at an area of rough and broken ice, but the light was poor and, with the weather deteriorating rapidly, we hurried back to camp. The next morning I woke to the din of a blizzard raging outside. That was expected. But there was another noise too — a quiet, persistent buzz. Still wrapped snugly in my sleeping-bag, I opened one eye, looking for the source. Straight above me glowed the two-centimetre blue arc of a continuous static discharge. The dry snow drift whipping over the fibreglass van was building up a static charge and, inside, blue filaments danced between adjacent pieces of metal.

When I looked out the perspex dome in the roof, the drift was so thick that I could not see the large red living van parked only metres from us.

'It's like travelling in a train!' exclaimed George Hedanek from his bunk, referring to the way the shrieking wind buffeted and rocked the van. The wind speed at Mawson was measured at ninety-eight knots (181 km/h) and on the exposed plateau where we were it was even stronger. It forced drift through every crack and pinhole in the van and the gear under my bed became encased in snow. We plugged the holes as best we could by stamping snow against them or using paper towel and tissues.

I was recording all this in my diary when I was interrupted by a visit from Dave. When he unlatched the door, the wind caught it and flung it open, slamming it against a gas cylinder on the landing. Drift poured in as he struggled to shut the door and George and I rushed to help him. The three of us had a horrendous time trying to get the door closed against the might of the wind and we were hampered by drift packing around the inside of the door frame. I went out to try and tie back the flailing power cord which kept catching in the top of the door. The hood of my coat was blown back and within a minute I had to come inside because my bare head, caked in drift, was in pain and I felt sick. George and Dave vainly tried to shut the door.

'We'll have to get out! We'll have to move!' George shouted to me above the howling wind.

'No!' I protested. 'We must get it shut. Everything will get buried in here if we leave!'

I felt too sick to help and, as there was not room for three at the door, I sat watching, silently praying they would get it shut. The door's hinges had bent when it blew open, but by persevering and with Dave working from the outside, they managed to get it almost closed and George jammed an ice axe through the handle to hold it in place.

Dave left with a rope he had borrowed from us to make a safety line to where the dogs were tethered. He gave up this plan, though, when the forty-metre coil of climbing rope was wrenched from his hands by the wind and lost in the maelstrom.

George and I still had the problem of drift streaming in through the gap around the door, so I stuffed paper towel in it, then turned to face the mess inside. There was fifteen centimetres of snow in the cold porch and a thick white layer covered the stove, shelves, books, sleeping-bags, clothes — everything.

Right: The replica of Mawson's half-sled

Above: Mawson at Mertz's 'grave'

We spent the next few hours scraping and brushing the snow into a large pile in the doorway and drying things out. I noted that 'it was a nasty experience and one I do not want repeated'. Overnight a lot of the snow melted and in the morning a couple of centimetres of water covered the floor. I bailed most of our indoor pool into the garbage can.

John Peiniger had also run into problems in the blizzard when he became lost while returning from the generator van to his living van. He crawled through the four-metre gap between it and a fuel sled without being able to see either. After some time without finding anything, he realised he had gone too far and decided to turn back. John stayed on all fours and crawled backwards, keeping himself orientated to the wind so as not to lose direction. He eventually bumped into the stake at one end of the dog line, worked out where he was and found his way to safety. It had taken

nearly an hour and a half for him to travel about two hundred metres.

When the blizzard died away we continued the filming. We normally rose at 7.00 am and after breakfast Liz would put on our makeup — blistered faces and cracked lips. The extra 'skin' on our lips was water soluble, so we could not eat or drink until after the required scene was shot. The filming was far more involved

and time-consuming than I had imagined and it was usually between midnight and 2.00 am before we went to bed.

The manhauling harness I used when we acted out Mawson's and Mertz's return journey had belonged to Eric Webb, the magnetician of the AAE. Along with Bob Bage and Frank Hurley, Webb had manhauled to within eighty kilometres of the south magnetic pole in December 1912. Objectively, the harness was only an old piece of stout canvas, but for me it held a certain mystique.

The time now came for Mertz's death sequence where I had to throw a fit. After doing the scene ten or more times — for practice, for shots with various lenses and angles, then for sound — I became tired of 'dying'. Two days later we dug my grave and built a snow-block cairn. I played Mertz's part to the end and climbed into a sleeping-bag in the hole. Inside the leather bag it was pitch black and the carbon

Left: Liz's makeup on 'Mertz'

56

dioxide level quickly rose, making me breathe rapidly. Dave waited until the blowing ground-drift partly buried me before he filmed 'Mawson' placing a cross on top of the snow cairn, then reading:

'I am the resurrection and the life,' saith the Lord. 'He that believeth in me, though he were dead, yet shall he live. And whoever liveth and believeth in me shall never die.'

Lying still in the darkness, I reflected how few people would have heard the burial service read over them! Many in such a situation, I considered, would have given anything for the opportunity to have heard those words — and to have accepted the offer that goes with them! 'Had Mertz committed his life to Jesus Christ?' I wondered. I was thankful I had.

Filming continued with Mawson's lone, tenacious striving for survival and I set about looking for suitable crevasses to film Ninnis's fatal accident and Mawson's fall. An arguably unhealthy appetite for crevasses

had developed in me since the exciting experience with the fuel sleds and I had come to that point — of madness according to some — where my sense of adventure overcame my sense of self-preservation. George and I were flown over the ice on the eastern side of Mt Henderson in helicopters and I chose promising-looking slots.

After landing and knocking a hole in the lid of the crevasse, I would leave George to

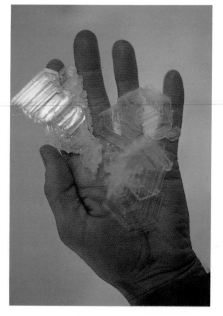

Above: 'Mawson' tows the half-sled

stand watch while, attached to a climbing rope, I descended a caving ladder into another world. A cold blue light radiated from the ice walls and there was no need for a torch. No sound or breath of wind penetrated to distract my senses from concentrating on the surrounding beauty. Time mattered little here and there seemed to be an eternity for the slow growth of ice crystals: individual water molecules, floating in the dry, frigid air, locked into regular arrangements forming exquisite hexagonal plates of ice which grew together and hung like faceted stalagtites. In a snow-filled crevasse, I crawled through a bright tunnel, its circumference lined with transparent crystals that tinkled down like fine glass as I brushed past towards a sparkling chamber.

The largest of the crevasses I ventured into was twelve to fifteen metres wide and, after an initial three-metre drop onto a 'ceiling' of ice, I edged down a steep slope, cutting steps with

my ice axe before abseiling off its overhanging brink. Two metres down I landed on the edge of a 'floor'. Back under the ceiling I had come off was a second floor, three metres below me again and between where I stood and this lower floor yawned a deep, dark hole. Vertical fissures — smaller crevices leading off the main one — split the smooth sides of the crevasse. The 'floors' were made of jumbled blocks of snow and ice up to three metres across which had obviously been the roof at one stage. Yes, it was possible that the present roof could fall on me at any moment, though this was unlikely and I thought it was worth the risk to be able to stand inside such a grotto.

Two days later, Paul was filmed falling through the roof of this cavern. The lid was so solid and thick that it took George some time to dig through it so the action could begin. Inside the crevasse I kept quiet as Dave began filming and Liz recorded sound. Paul plummeted to the end of his harness rope, spun giddily

and started hauling himself up the rope.

'The watch!' Dave yelled despairingly, making me jump in fright. There on 'Mawson's' grasping arm gleamed a digital watch — hardly the sort of timepiece worn by early Antarctic explorers! Such incidents added humour — and frustration — to our efforts.

The crevasse scenes over, I went back to Mawson to clear up unfinished work and prepare for returning to Australia. I had thoroughly enjoyed the filming and had gained an insight not only into film-making but also some of the difficulties and deprivations of early expeditions.

On 25 February, the last supply vessel for the season arrived. A visiting ship still filled me with excitement and I stood outside with the rest of Mawson to watch *Nanok S* approach. As it sailed down Kista Strait, everyone's attention was fixed on the end of West Arm where half-a-dozen two-hundred-litre drums of ATK,

strapped with explosives, erupted in a billowing ball of orange flame. This form of salutation is now banned, but it certainly enlivened the occasion!

The majority of the 1981 winterers were to leave on *Nella Dan* which had been carrying out geoscience work since leaving Mawson on 27 January. At 8.00 am on 2 March, I was woken by Paul's voice calling down the hallway, 'If there's anyone who wants to go home, be down by the LARCs with your gear in an hour.' Cheers rang out from the dongas and everyone hurriedly dressed and began carting bags. The usual confusion reigned and it was midday before we left. The extra time gave Bob Yeoman and Norm Jones the opportunity to varnish the toilet seats. 'After all,' said Norm, 'they haven't been done all year!'

I left on the last LARC wearing old overalls and a garbage bag to protect myself from the farewellers who threw flour and water bombs. Motor-

ing out to *Nella* in Kista Strait, I felt regret at leaving Mawson after enjoying a great year. However, I knew others were sick of the place and were eager to get home.

The return voyage was uneventful and we sailed up the Derwent River to Hobart on the pleasantly sunny morning of 15 March 1982. I stared at the trees covering the hills — things only imagined or recalled in pictures over the last fourteen months. Something else I was not used to was speed. When my brother drove me from the wharf I felt nervous because we seemed to be flying along, though the car was doing less than sixty kilometres per hour. It did not take long before I once again became accustomed to travelling at a pace faster than that of a bull-dozer or dog sled. That afternoon I enjoyed the taste of fresh grapes, blackberries and milk, and the feel of my bare feet in the warm sand of a beach.

4
Autumn traverse

CAPTAIN WILLIAMS, Master of the Canadian vessel *Lady Franklin*, handed me a 'Polar Certificate' which declared 'to all Seal and Penguin that: R.K. Butler hath crossed the Antarctic Circle, 30 January 1984.' I walked to the the rail and watched the Adelie penguins grouped on ice floes as the ship approached Davis, our first port of call on my second trip south. My destination this time was Casey.

After returning from Mawson, I had continued to work for the Antarctic Division which had moved from Melbourne to Kingston, south of Hobart. When my term of employment ran out, there seemed good reason to reapply to go south again. Like so many past expeditioners, I was enchanted with Antarctica and resolved to return. At Casey I was to go on the major traverses inland and deploy three automatic weather stations. They were an upgraded version of the AWS I had established south-west of Mawson.

Nearly all the voyage was

under grey skies but, as we passed through a maze of icebergs to reach Davis, the welcome sun shone on the mainland. We dropped anchor around 9.30 am and after lunch I stood on the deck watching most of the passengers going ashore on the LARCs. An inflatable boat came alongside the ship and its two passengers climbed aboard. They were Dr David Lewis and a companion, and I showed them up to the captain. In 1972-73, Dr Lewis became the first person to sail single-handed to Antarctica and had just spent the winter of 1983 with five others at the Rauer Islands off Davis on the yacht, *Dick Smith Explorer*. This was now moored at Davis and Dr Lewis had come out to ask about current ice conditions. He thought the yacht might have to follow *Lady Franklin* through the pack ice to reach the open ocean, but on learning that there was only light pack, *Explorer* sailed later that afternoon.

Those travelling on *Lady Franklin* were allowed to visit Davis again the following day while cargo was unloaded. I

went for a walk to Lake Dingle, one of the many lakes in the Vestfold Hills. In common with a number of others in these hills, it is saline. Some are so salty they do not even freeze in winter. Raised beaches along some of the hillsides which show where sea and land once met is another interesting feature of the Vestfolds. Walking back to Davis to rejoin the ship, I enjoyed the sunshine, the stillness and the silence of that cold, rocky desert after the motion and noise of the ship. At ten past eleven that night we weighed anchor, sailed out between the many 'bergs, and headed for Casey. The following afternoon, *Lady Franklin* overtook *Dick Smith Explorer* which looked picturesque under sail, but tiny as it tacked past mountainous tabular icebergs.

Approaching Casey on 5 February, the ship nudged through the pack ice and I joined the other passengers and took in the magical scenery about us.

Opposite: Casey, with the new station buildings behind

Here and there on the floes stood emperor and Adelie penguins warming themselves in the sunshine. Weddell and leopard seals raised their sleepy heads from the ice and either ignored the ship and continued snoozing or wriggled to the edge of their floe and slipped into the water. Aqua moats surrounded the icebergs and cruising past these weathered bastions revealed deep blues in the cracks and caves. In the evening, the setting sun cast an orange pathway across the coloured water and this strange world floated in darkening twilight.

The ship entered Newcomb Bay and was greeted by those at Casey with the traditional explosion. We anchored at 11.28 pm and a barge came out to pick up the mail. It was rigged with a sail and its crew were dressed as pirates. They collected their booty and happily left for the shore.

At seven the next morning, I boarded a LARC to Casey where I met my predecessor,

Left: *Lady Franklin* moored at Davis

Lex Harris, who showed me around. He demonstrated the experiments I was to look after and the equipment I would be running and maintaining on traverse. I was pleased to renew two old acquaintances from my year at Mawson — George Hedanek had spent 1983 at Casey and Bob Yeoman was to winter at the base during the coming year.

The port of Casey became busier on 9 February when *Nanok S* arrived with more mail, stores, equipment and the last of the 1984 wintering expeditions. *Lady Franklin* sailed the following evening, taking home the 1983 crew. Over the next hectic forty-eight hours, the days were spent unloading and the nights with writing letters home. On the afternoon of 12 February, I watched the last physical contact we would have with the rest of the world for the next nine months sail away. In one way I was glad to see it go as the base could now settle down to a normal routine.

Above and right: Unloading and disembarking on a LARC

Casey station

There had been few opportunities to look around Casey and its surroundings during the full days that the ships were in. I found the station quite different to Mawson, the most distinguishing feature being the 'tunnel' which joined the buildings together and proved convenient in bad weather. There were no water restrictions as at Mawson and the chemical toilets, while not without their own idiosyncrasies, seemed more civilised than those at Mawson. The dongas were similar, but nearly half of them had no windows and these were known as 'bat caves'. In my 'cave', a former occupant had installed a small vent in the roof which could channel in fresh air. This was useful, as I found the dongas to be too stuffy. I have woken in the middle of the night, however, and discovered I was being snowed upon!

There were thirty of us, all men, spending the winter at Casey, including a guest scien-

Left: Moulting Adelie penguins
Above: Autumn or Fall traverse leaving

tist from the People's Republic of China. Qin Dahe was a glaciologist and I got to know him well as we shared the same work area. During the unloading I was surprised to discover that he did not know how to drive. I immediately gave him his first practical lesson after describing the function of the controls as simply as I could. The vehicle's 'sudden' clutch and the very bumpy roads were not conducive to learning and we bounced along in first gear. A number of lessons and instructors later he graduated, but I will always remember his initial approach to the application of the brake pedal: it was digital in nature — either fully on or fully off!

With the ships gone, many people directed their efforts into preparations for the first, the autumn, traverse which was scheduled to leave in early March. Besides the six who would actually be on the traverse, the work of overhauling equipment and assembling the required stores involved the carpenter, plumber, electrician, radio technicians, mechanics,

doctor and cook. Their assistance was essential and, after the long hours they put in, they were glad to see us go!

On 8 March, under a dark sky and with the wind blowing clouds of drift, we left Casey and headed south. I was pleased to be going away and venturing inland. There were four tractor trains using three Caterpillar D5 bulldozers plus a more powerful and brand new D7 called *Jane* as prime movers to tow ten sleds. On two of the sleds were living vans, named *Flash* and *Gordon*, with a generator/workshop van behind each. The other sleds carried fuel and a shipping container with the bulk of our food.

Occupying *Flash* were Rik Thwaites, the glaciologist and traverse leader, with Russell Brand and Andy Wood, the diesel mechanics or 'diesos' for short. I was sharing *Gordon* with Gary Burton, the head mechanic and Jim Clarke, the surveyor.

Living in *Gordon* was a far cry from the tents of the early explorers. The outside

door led into a small cold porch and a second door into the body of the van. At the front end, a ladder led up to a roof hatch and three bunks were squeezed between floor and ceiling with curtains across them for privacy. Opposite was all the scientific instrumentation and communication gear, while the rear half was taken up with the cooking and eating area. The numerous cupboards were full of tinned food, though we generally ate frozen meat and vegetables from the shipping container. We considered our refrigerator to be anywhere outside the door.

Water was obtained from a snow melter in the generator van. The melter consisted of a two-hundred-litre drum with a heating element. It also provided water for a recent innovation — a shower! While this was excessive luxury by the standards of earlier expeditions, it was not without problems: its drain, a hole in one corner of the floor, occasionally

Above: Inside *Gordon* van
Left: Jim Clarke filling the bucket for the snow melter

required built-up ice to be
smashed out of it and when
showering it was wise to partially cover the drain as a chill
– 40 °C breeze whistling around
you was most unwelcome!

After travelling 170
kilometres across Law Dome
from Casey, we descended the
slope into a wide valley commonly called 'The Trench'
which separates the Dome and
the Antarctic plateau. Our
major objective was to lay a
fuel depot at a point called
GC37, roughly halfway along
the route we would be taking
on the spring traverse. As we
hauled out of The Trench, we
began to ascend the huge dome
of ice which covers the Antarctic continent. Even though
Antarctica's central plateau
receives little more precipita-
tion than the Sahara Desert, the
snow which has accumulated
there has built up to be over
four kilometres thick. Under its
own weight, the snow com-
pacts into ice which flows
slowly out toward the coast,
breaking off as icebergs.

Above: Refuelling at night
Right: Travelling over the snowy plateau

The main purpose of the glaciological traverse program was to help build up a picture of the speed, direction and amount of ice flowing off Antarctica in the Wilkes Land region. We were to use satellite survey equipment to remeasure the position of established markers in the spreading icecap. By finding the new position of a marker, we could determine how fast and in what direction the surrounding ice was moving. Two or three days at a time were spent at each ice movement station recording data received from satellites which passed overhead. We stopped at three of these stations during the autumn traverse.

For the first three weeks I stayed in *Gordon* during the day and ran the ice radar. This produced a photographic record of ice depth, the result appearing as a cross-section of the icecap along the length of the film. While I measured the icecap's depths, its surface, covered with sastrugi and small crescent-shaped dunes of soft drift, extended endlessly in every direction. Its utter emptiness and remoteness, the mere fact that we were so far from anyone or anything, held a certain fascination for me.

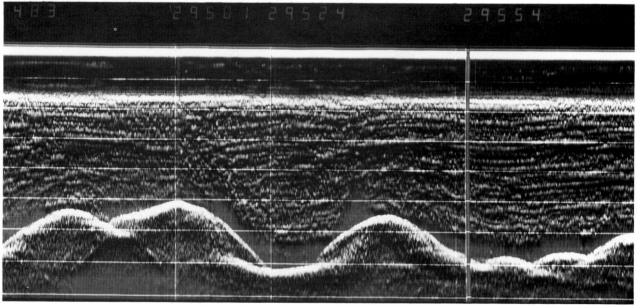

'Five degrees to your left, Russell,' Jim directed over the radio. 'You should be able to see the next cane soon.' Jim was using the radar in *Flash* to navigate while the others drove the 'dozers. We stopped at each marker cane and put in a new cane alongside the existing one. The accumulation of snow gradually buries the canes and the heights of both the new and old ones were recorded so that annual snowfall figures could be calculated. The canes were identified with a numbered tag and each had a drink can jammed onto it to improve the reflection on the navigation radar. When the supply of cans began to run short, Rik would encourage us to 'drink for science'.

On 30 March I took over driving Rik's bulldozer, *Wendy*. That day was overcast, producing white-out conditions, and I found the only way I could tell I was moving was by watching the 'dozer tracks and feeling the bumps when running over sastrugi. It was a weird experience to be travelling yet not be able to see the ground moving past or a horizon — just a sea of shadowless white. At one stage it took a call from Jim to point out that I was bogged. Because there was nothing to see outside to indicate I was stopped and as the tracks were still moving, I did not realise the 'dozer was stationary and digging itself into the snow! That afternoon the going was rough over the sastrugi and I slowed down to give the living van a smoother ride. Inside it you were pitched about terribly and had to hang on tight or get hurt. Working in the van was more than difficult.

'I can see the next cane,' I

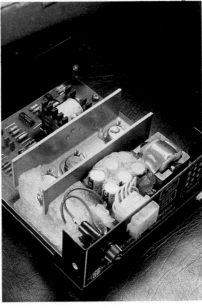

Top left: Working the ice radar
Left: Ice radar film showing a variation in ice thickness of 845 to 1,208 metres
Top right: Measuring canes
Right: Problems! Iced-up voltage converter and air filter

informed Jim over the radio. 'It's a few hundred metres away with only about a metre of it poking above the snow.'

'According to the route guide it's supposed to be a fibreglass pole,' he replied, 'and I don't think we should be on it yet.' I rechecked: the stick had vanished, but with hard staring I found it again. 'They must pop up and down out of the snow,' I thought. Over a kilometre later, we reached my one-metre cane — a pole three metres high! On the plateau, it is hard to judge distances and the size of objects without something to scale them by.

Our expectations of poor weather at this time of year were justified. We experienced many days of thick, blowing drift and occasionally blizzard conditions which forced us to remain camped and we would have a 'blizz day', maintaining gear or relaxing. Navigating in poor weather was difficult for a variety of reasons. Sastrugi gave reflections on the radar screen similar to canes which were impossible to spot visually if there was drift blowing. Frost on the inside of the 'dozer windows further hampered visibility and often the only clear areas were narrow strips along the heating elements on the glass.

The limitations of the radar and regular poor visibility were not the only navigational difficulties. To accurately determine our bearings, magnetic compasses could not be depended on. Because the earth's north and south magnetic poles do not lie over the North and South Pole (the geographic poles) but are offset from them, compasses generally do not point exactly north-south. The south magnetic pole was first reached in January 1909 by Douglas Mawson, Edgeworth David and Alistair

Left: Jim Clarke using an astrocompass for navigation
Right: Camp at dawn

Mackay (from Shackleton's 1907-1909 Antarctic expedition). By 1984 it had moved off Antarctica to be over the ocean and was some 1,300 kilometres east of Casey. A compass needle indicating north at Casey was pointing westwards and this error increased in an uncertain way when moving inland, making a compass unreliable. We obtained true bearings using an astrocompass and the sun. This was a quick, reliable method, only failing on heavily overcast days.

We continued south to GC37 at 70° 9.3′ S, 111° 50.1′ E and celebrated reaching our turnaround point on 6 April with a turkey dinner. The following day, in bitter conditions, we unloaded 114 two-hundred-litre drums of fuel that would be picked up on the spring traverse. The dump was marked out with canes as the drums would probably be buried by drifting snow before we returned. With the depot established, the loads on the trip back would be lighter, but now a formidable problem faced us: the D7 had broken down. The automatic transmission fluid was so thick in the cold that the pump failed in the unequal struggle. The oil, quite runny at 'normal' temperatures, had the consistency of vegemite in the minus forties. A new product to us, it was obviously not suited for Antarctic use and our other 'dozer with automatic transmission was having no difficulties.

Towing *Jane* would have caused more damage, so it was clear she would have to be carried. Andy dug a ramp into the snow, a sled was backed into it and *Jane* was winched on and chained down. We started the homeward journey on 9 April with a vehicle which weighed nearly twenty-three tonnes on a sled designed to

carry ten tonnes. We were courting trouble but had little choice and, in a foretaste of what was to come, the sled runner chains broke on the first attempt to shift the D7.

Our next major mechanical problem occurred two days later when *Wendy's* motor overheated. The cause was a failed harmonic balancer, the pulley which the fan and alternator run off. Over a day of unenviable work lay ahead for Gary, Russell and Andy. All the work had to be done in the weather with only a tarpaulin as a screen against the twenty-five knot (46 km/h), − 45°C wind in which exposed flesh could freeze within one minute. Nuts and washers were easily dropped in the snow from cold, gloved hands and the diesos worked for as long as they could tolerate before retreating into the generator van to warm up.

At some stage during the trip, we all suffered frostnip to fingers or cheeks. This occurs when a small area of skin freezes and it appears as a white patch. Frostbite is more

severe and involves the freezing of the tissue underneath the skin as well. Usually beginning in fingers or toes, it may extend up the limb. Two of my fingers had turned white and lost all feeling the day we had put out the fuel dump. As they slowly thawed, the pain was intense and it felt like I was holding them in a flame. They were tender for a couple of days and the skin on my fingertips died and gradually peeled off.

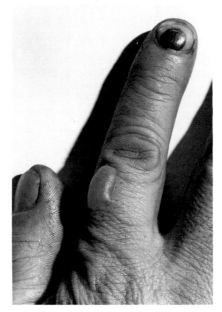

During the stop to repair *Wendy*, I examined the latest fault in a continuing series of electronic breakdowns. I found a protection circuit which kept shutting down *Gordon's* radar was being triggered by the inability of an electric motor to rotate the antenna. The antenna bearings had stiffened in temperatures now approaching − 50°C, but hopefully they would free up again with warmer weather.

On our way again, soft conditions regularly bogged the 'dozers and we had to double-haul the sleds which meant taking some of them ahead, returning for the others, towing them several kilometres past the first ones and so on in a leap-frog fashion. The vehicles then travelled three times the distance we actually made in one day and this was kept up all the way back to Casey. The D7 was a heavy load which often needed two of the D5s pulling in tandem to haul it.

Above: The mechanics doing engine repairs at -45°C
Left: Gary Burton's finger, blistered from sustained contact with metal at -20°C

Late in the afternoon of 20 April, we were maintaining our persistent drive homewards. The sky was clear, but the sun had set and when I looked out the front window of *Gordon* it was difficult to see past the towing 'dozer because of the dense layer of drift being carried by the wind. Suddenly there was a cry over the radio from Russell: 'Gary, stop!' By the urgency in his voice I knew there was something seriously wrong: *Flash*, with Rik inside, had fallen over.

Flash had ridden up on some large sastrugi and fallen off the sled runner assemblies which it sat on. The train of sleds remained linked, though, because the runners were still connected to *Wendy* in front and the generator van behind. This, together with the rough surface and bad visibility, meant Gary was oblivious to the accident and kept on driving. Russell was travelling behind and raised the alarm, but not before the generator sled had smashed into the back of the living van now lying on the snow. The van landed with

its door facing downwards and Russell had to help Rik out through the roof hatch.

Andy towed Jim and I in *Gordon* back to the accident and Jim brought Rik inside. Although dazed, Rik was able to tell me what had happened to him. He had been looking for a cane from the roof hatch when Gary warned him of some rough sastrugi, so he climbed down the ladder and hung on. He said the van had tilted

alarmingly — past the angle that makes you wonder if it's going to tip — until it crashed on its side with everything flying off shelves and out of cupboards. He was thrown into one of the bunks and was struck on the head by what we assumed was one of the radio transceivers. Fortunately, he had been wearing his sheepskin hat which softened the blow. Gary was upset because Rik had been hurt and he felt responsible, but no-one would have guessed that such an accident might occur.

Flash was winched upright and I replaced the power inlet which had been demolished. The inside of the van was chaotic. The cupboards had been flung open and their contents now filled the beds and corridor along with the dinner Rik had been cooking in the oven. A quick cleanup was carried out to bring the van to a habitable state for the night.

Rik was still dazed and we took regular checks of his

Above: Towing out a bogged D5 bulldozer
Left: Chaos inside *Flash* van

75

pulse, the size of his pupils and other vital signs. We urgently wanted the doctor's advice, head injuries always being potentially serious, but were unable to contact Casey on that night's radio sked because of poor atmospheric conditions. We were truly on our own in this situation and would have to rely on limited resources and ingenuity for both the medical and mechanical problems. I realised the remoteness which I found attractive was now a threat.

In the morning, the weather had changed little from the previous day with the temperature at −35°C and a thirty to forty knot (56-74 km/h) wind keeping the obscuring drift rushing past us. Despite the temperature, the drift melted on clothes and faces, then refroze in a layer of ice. The diesos worked in this, putting *Flash* back on the sled runners. The task would normally have been done using a crane, but now they had to improvise. Andy and Russell positioned their bulldozers either side of *Flash* and raised it well off the

ground using the bottom edge of their 'dozer blades. This tricky operation required some careful lining up and co-ordinated lifting and during the first attempt the van slipped from one blade, shearing off the power inlet again. They slowly lowered the van after Gary had accurately positioned the sled underneath it with a hand winch.

During the day I unsuccessfully radioed Casey every two hours and even tried calling Davis and Mawson in the hope we could make contact. It was not until that night that I heard a reply to my call and could at last speak with Casey's doctor, Bruce Adam. I explained Rik's injury.

'OK, I want you to take his boots off,' Bruce said.

'Take his boots off?' I questioned. This seemed a strange place to start examining head injuries and I wondered if I was the target of a practical joke.

'Yes, that's right. Then run your thumb along the sole of his foot and tell me if his toes curl up or down,' he answered. The result was toes down, a

simple test that confirmed there was no pressure on his brain from internal bleeding. Along with the favourable observations we had made of Rik, this greatly relieved Bruce's concern, not to mention that of Rik, Gary and the rest of us.

Our laboured journey restarted on 22 April and was continually slowed by broken winch cables, tow bars, chains and fittings. The front of the sled carrying the D7 collapsed under the strain and required the replacement of a snapped kingpin. Close inspection of the sled revealed large fatigue cracks around the kingpins in the steel cross members and other damage, but little could be done to repair this and we had to press on. 'Only ten days to go!' Gary repeated daily and the run of minor breakdowns put truth into his joke.

Russell called our attention to the sunrise one morning as we were about to move off. The sky was overcast except for a slit along the eastern horizon and from this the huge red beam of a solar pillar shone like a searchlight under the grey clouds. The beauty of this bright ray was striking and refreshing for me.

Rik had planned to meet a resupply traverse from Casey on Law Dome and then undertake the first winter traverse. This was thwarted by an unserviceable vehicle at Casey and we continued across the Dome towards base. Our first traverse ended on Saturday 5 May and had proved a trial of the equipment and ourselves. It had taken patience and perseverance from all of us and I knew I was not the only one relieved to be safely back when friends welcomed us as we descended the slope to Casey, climbed over eight weeks previously.

Above: Lowering *Flash* back onto its sled
Right: A solar pillar

5
Midwinter at Casey

THE NEXT MORNING, I left most of Casey asleep and walked off through lightly falling snow to the sea near Kilby Island. In the muted light there was an atmosphere of calmness and peace. Where the sea ice had been blown away by strong wind, the placid water was matted with snowflakes which lay paralysed and unmelting as the surface refroze. The tensions and cares of the past two months faded away as I soaked in the tranquility of the surroundings. Two snow petrels flew along the frosty cliff at the side of the island, turned about me with a swish of wings and sheered away, low across the water.

The week following my day of relaxation was taken up with repairs and maintenance of gear for the first winter traverse which had to leave as soon as possible. The main job was to repair the navigation radar antenna so it would not freeze again. Trevor Lloyd, the senior radio technical officer, and I spent uncomfortable hours perched on the scaffold above

Gordon. It was a battle dismantling and working on the antenna while hanging on and trying to keep out snow and we inevitably dropped a screw or washer which landed invisibly in the soft powder snow below. The bearings were fair, but someone had spread a lot of grease around them which was thick even then at −15°C. No wonder the antenna had not rotated at −45°C! On wiping out the grease, it turned far more freely.

I farewelled the first winter traverse on 14 May. It was also troubled with more than its fair share of difficulties. The party had to sit out some bad weather and then the gearbox of *Gentle Ben* failed, forcing them to return. On their arrival after a brief trip of fourteen days, two out of two traverses had come back to Casey with a bulldozer on a sled!

Their return was untimely for me because I was slushy of the week. Helping Bill Robinson the cook prepare meals and serve them, washing up and cleaning the mess was a break from my usual work, but

I did not enjoy keeping up with Bill's constant demand for peeled potatoes! He had Sundays off, so I was required to show my skill as a master chef at the end of the week. Ably assisted by the new slushy, Andy Wood, I fed the masses to their satisfaction and then relaxed in front of the Sunday night movie.

Soon after returning to my normal work, I decided to test out the new mast design for the automatic weather stations by erecting one inland at Lanyon Junction, fifteen kilometres as the skua flies from Casey. Four of us set off one morning and on the way were treated to a panorama of snowy hills tinted orange by the low winter sun that also highlighted the vertical faces of icebergs set in the grey-blue sea ice. We arrived at Lanyon and soon became warm digging the metre-deep holes for the mast and guy anchors. Picks and mattocks were needed to cut through layers of ice which had formed during the summer seasons when the surface melts and refreezes.

The lack of wind while

putting up the mast made the job fairly comfortable with the temperature at – 14 °C. The weather we experienced that June was average for Casey and the Met boys' monthly weather summary read:

Mean temperature: -15.7 °C,
1.8 °C < average
Highest maximum: — 4.0 °C on 1st
Lowest minimum: -30.3 °C on 8th
Mean maximum: -12.5 °C,
2.5 °C < average

Mean minimum: -19.0 °C,
1.2 °C < average
Mean station level pressure:
982.2 hPa
Highest station level pressure:
999.0 hPa on 5th
Lowest station level pressure:
957.7 hPa on 13th
Mean wind speed: 8.3 knots
(15 km/h)
Maximum wind gust: 73 knots
(135 km/h)
Days of strong winds (22-33
knots, 41-61 km/h): 9 days

Days of gale force winds
(≥ 34 knots, 63 km/h): 5 days
Total measurable snowfall:
36.9 mm
Days of snowfall: 20 days
Mean daily sunshine hours:
0.2 hours

A very average June (yawn).

Above: Fourteen-hour star trail taken in the middle of winter
Below: Met balloon ascending from Casey

June was the month with the longest nights. Because Casey lies just outside the Antarctic Circle we did not lose the sun completely but, living at the limit of its precincts, it only spilled its rays over the northern skyline during the core of each day.

The shortest day of the year approached and Bill was the busiest of those preparing for the midwinter celebrations as he cooked and assembled a lavish variety of dishes for his midwinter banquet. Eric Szworak, the Met technician, spent hours doing the design, calligraphy and printing the photographs for the menu, and our maintenance electrician, Ray Etherington, put his fertile mind to work writing a new play about Snow White when the official Cinderella script could not be found.

The winter solstice, 21 June, arrived and the mess was adorned with flags, balloons, streamers, Antarctic pictures and lights. The centrepiece of the decorations was a wall created by stacking blocks of ice coloured with dyes, and all the seafood was arranged on and around this. The settings on the tables had so much cutlery there seemed little room for plates and the seven-course meal started at 3.00 pm and went on and on. The night's festivities flowed on into the morning and it was just as well the following day had been declared a public holiday as some people needed the time to recover! This short period of time off for joviality provided a good break for us after the constant routine of work.

One week after midwinter, the second winter traverse left Casey and continued the tradition of suffering poor weather and a headache with a vehicle.

Top and centre: The icewall and food for the midwinter dinner
Left: The midwinter play

Above: Towing the watercart

No 'dozer returned on a sled this time but *Kingston*, the D5 involved with the sleds in the crevasse at Mawson, partially fell into a slot and had to be dug out. The hazard of crevasses was one we did not have to face on the longer trips because the autumn and spring traverse routes were over thick ice. This trip achieved a lot more than the previous one and all returned safely on 23 July.

I did not have to leave Casey to have trouble with vehicles. One morning I faced a bulldozer cab heater belching flame. The heater was mounted externally on the 'dozer used to tow the water cart from the meltlake to Casey's water tanks and I had discovered flames spouting from its exhaust. My efforts to extinguish the blaze by attempting to starve it of air and fuel had been fruitless and I had to let it burn itself out. Later in the day, as part of my nightwatch duties, my return from the rubbish run was thwarted by an unreliable little tractor called *Maria*. I trudged up the hill and found a dieso, Garry Barclay.

'*Maria*'s clutch is jammed down again,' I explained.

'You must be careful not to push it too far in,' he said, picking up a large screwdriver. Back at the immobile machine he prodded deep into its internals.

'It's okay now. How about a tow up the hill?' I asked hopefully. 'I slipped backwards from halfway on the last attempt.'

'No, just give it curry! You should make it,' he answered. I reversed, then charged up the rough slope, barely managing to hold on as the tractor bucked and slipped over the rocks and snow until reaching the top.

Blackouts occurred occasionally and could be a real problem. One of the most inconvenient blackouts had occurred in May. After a day of erratically blowing wind it suddenly strengthened at 2.30 in the morning and fifteen minutes later everyone was shocked into a state of semi-consciousness by the clanging of the fire alarm bells. We hastily dressed ready for outside work and staggered up the tunnel to the assembly

point at Radio. The tunnel was filled with the noise of the screaming wind, measured at over 100 knots (185 km/h). The alarm had been triggered in the transmitter building and to reach it meant a drive of around two kilometres. Outside, the visibility was down to a couple of metres and there was every chance a vehicle would be lost, if not blown over, so it was decided the trip was not a particularly good idea.

A temperature sensor located in the transmitter building with a remote readout in Radio showed a normal reading, so we assumed it was a false alarm. Just as people started to head off for bed, the wind reached a peak of 110 knots (204 km/h) and all the lights went out — a total power failure. The lucky people who were responsible for the generators braced themselves, stepped out into the shrieking, swirling blackness and fought their way across to the powerhouse.

They had the power back on by 3.30 am and after all the excitement I joined a number of others in the mess and socialised before wandering off to bed again.

While blizzards had some effect on work, they did not stop it altogether. A blizzard meant that the builders could not reach the new station to work, but it was business as usual for the diesos, carpenter and plumber. They hung onto the rope lines that guided the way to their workshops. The Met men also went out in any weather for some of their measurements, although when the wind reached around eighty knots (148 km/h), it became pointless to launch a radiosonde balloon because it would be swept away and bounce along the ground. My work arrangements in bad weather were quite comfortable and with a number of others I wore the stigma of 'tunnel dweller'. The tunnel joined the main building line together, providing shelter and so freedom and ease of getting between dongas, the mess and your workplace.

Casey had been built above ground level with the tunnel facing the prevailing easterly wind to allow the wind to blow underneath and keep the lee side of the buildings free from snow drifts. During a good blow, all of Casey shook and rattled incessantly despite being supported by a mass of scaffold pipes and being guyed down with steel cables. In my workshop, storage cabinet drawers vibrated open, spilling their contents of screws and components onto the floor.

Since returning from the autumn traverse I had been busy in this workshop constructing the weather stations.

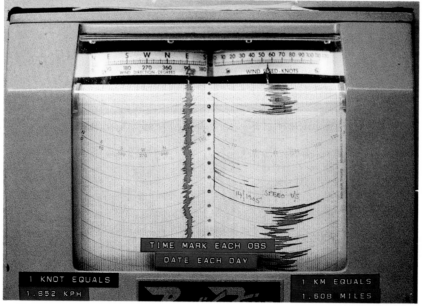

Top: Andy Wood in the tunnel after a blizzard
Left: A blown-down antenna wire interrupted this record

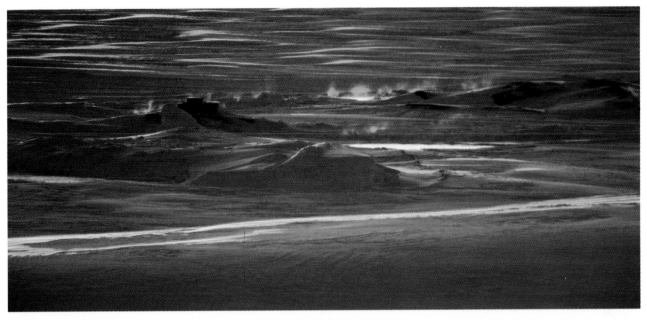

Above: Frost smoke 'steaming' from relatively warm sea water
Below: Frost flowers growing around a tide crack

The plan had been for all three to be built and tested before leaving Australia, but I was only now putting together the printed circuit boards and calibrating them. The project was a victim of the Antarctic factor, suffering a run of setbacks. One such setback was when four of six special lead-acid batteries were accidentally smashed while being delivered to the science building. They had been broken within a few hundred metres of their destination after travelling safely for several thousand kilometres!

I was keen to see all three stations completed as originally intended despite being told by Glaciology section in Australia that the program could get by with only one. Other people volunteered to help and with their assistance the work gradually came nearer to completion.

Being busy made me appreciate more having Sundays off for a break and there was much of simple beauty to see about the base. Around the shoreline, the sea ice was broken from being raised and lowered by the tide and water would well up through these tide cracks in places. If it was calm and cold, this would produce frost smoke, a mist of ice crystals rising from the water which, being relatively much warmer than the air, 'steamed'. As the water froze, fragile clusters of ice crystals called frost flowers blossomed on its surface.

Whenever part of the sea ice on Newcomb Bay broke away, we could stand on its edge and view the watery landscape below that was normally hidden from our eyes. When Bruce discovered three jellyfish in the water I had to have a look.

Open water after a blizzard
has blown away the sea ice

The two largest were half a metre across and mauve in colour. On the bottom I saw anchor-ice growing on the rocks and clinging to tree-like pieces of seaweed and amongst this swam ice fish and a worm-like animal about half a metre long. I was intrigued by how slowly everything moved, the 'worm' in particular taking minutes to change its position. The ice I stood on was a dividing layer: above it had now been deserted by wildlife but below was still inhabited, the residents carrying on, albeit sedately.

On the opposite side of Newcomb Bay from Casey is the abandoned station of Wilkes, and Eric Szworak and I decided to visit there one Sunday. Wilkes was constructed in the 1956/57 austral summer by the USA for the International Geophysical Year of 1957/58 and was handed over to Australia in February 1959. Casey was built later and was opened on 19 February 1969 at which time Wilkes was vacated. We drove across to Wilkes in a Hagglunds and walked around the station. Most of the buildings were nearly buried by snow and this gradual burying was a major reason for building Casey.

The only way of getting into some of the buildings was via their roof hatches. I ventured through a couple of these, the first leading to a darkroom. On the top couple of shelves were film spools, spare light globes and bottles. I could not see what was further down because below this the room was full of ice, accumulated from snow drift that had come in around the roof hatch and melted over successive summers. In the mess there was more space and the cupboards, their curtains drawn back and draping down into the ice, still held jams, tea and matches. It gave me a strange feeling to be in this now deserted room, once the hub of many expeditions, with everything so ordinary and ready to be used. Yet it never would be and in the silence Antarctica slowly reclaimed it, locking it away in ice.

Above: Eric Szworak at the Wilkes transmitter building – one of the few not buried
Left: Rowan Butler in Wilkes mess which is half full of ice
Right: An arch in an iceberg

6
Spring traverse

IN EARLY AUGUST I WROTE all my Christmas cards. When the first ship arrived in mid-November I would be hundreds of kilometres from Casey, still heading south on the spring traverse. Station personnel were getting equipment and supplies ready for the four-month-long trip: Bill and a roster of assistants, for instance, spent evenings baking three hundred loaves of bread. There had to be more than enough food for our planned needs in case our return was delayed.

The departure date loomed closer and phone calls to and from home and friends became more important to me because inland, the only reliable communication would be via telex. I was hoping to be able to talk on the ham radio, but this depended on atmospheric conditions which had been variable during the year.

The schedule for building the automatic weather stations and installing the three sets of electronics in their metal drums was tight, and they were only put on air and tested in the week before we left. When the

results came from Australia, I was discouraged to learn that all were faulty. The night before leaving I was helped by Trevor Lloyd in tracing the problem. Our perseverance was rewarded when at 6.00 am we discovered a wiring error common to each unit. Pleased at finding this and with the deluded belief that my AWS troubles were now over, I snatched a couple of hours' sleep before we loaded the

weather stations and headed up to where the trains were being readied for leaving.

It was 15 September and the mandatory bad weather for a traverse send-off did not stop the friendly handshaking and farewelling, especially from those who would have left on a ship by the time we came back. 'Customs' was present to inspect our goods and we were issued with 'passports' so we could re-enter the Casey precincts on our return. When we drove away and the waving figures blurred and were lost to sight in the veil of drift, I breathed a sigh of relief that the frantic lead-up to the trip was over.

Except for Brian Baxter having replaced Gary Burton as the dieso in *Gordon*, it was the same crew as for the autumn traverse. The four trains were being towed by D5 bulldozers and during the next few days we travelled in good weather, only interrupted by banks of fog which built up hoarfrost on the vans and vehicles.

Left: Bread for the traverse
Top right: After a blizzard

On the summit of Law Dome we picked up drums of fuel left on the second traverse. They were already buried by snow and had to be dug out. That evening I received a telex from George Hedanek wishing us a successful traverse without blizzards or vehicle breakdowns. We certainly hoped that his wish would come true regarding the latter!

The first ice movement station and AWS site was at a position called A028, at 68° 24.4′ S, 112° 12.6′ E. We arrived there on 26 September after poor weather had cost us two days and soft conditions had forced us to double-haul. The weather then held up erecting the AWS mast for two days. When we were able to put it up the conditions were still not pleasant — the temperature was below −30°C and a twenty knot (37 km/h) wind blew drift over us. We made frequent trips to a nearby living van to warm up, especially when only thin gloves could be worn for the fiddly jobs. With the instruments on the mast, I connected the cabling to the

electronics drum which we buried with the battery box in a two-metre-deep trench downwind of the mast.

The next day I stood by the antenna and checked that the AWS was transmitting. It was not. Disheartened, I tracked the fault down to the battery box connector. It had been manufactured with its locating keyway for the plug on the opposite side to where it should have been and the

supply voltage had been applied in reverse. There were dozens of this kind of connector used in the weather stations and the only defective one had found its way into this critical spot!

I replaced a charred printed circuit board, exchanged the bad connector on the battery box and put the AWS on the air. My overnight hopes that it was now working were dashed when I received the news from head office: 'data confused'. The best course of action was to take the electronics drum with us, try to fix it and deploy it on the way home.

We continued southwards and I took over driving *Wendy* from Rik. I had little traffic to worry about and, like the others, I filled in time by reading. In good weather it was not difficult to read, take directions over the radio from the navigator and keep an eye out for canes, or the sleds in front if you were following directly behind someone. One day, engrossed in a book, I did not notice Brian stop ahead and ran straight into the back of

Gordon's generator van. I was moving slowly, but *Wendy* crushed the step on the rear landing before stalling. Extremely embarrassing, though I was not the only one to have an accident: other drivers had inadvertently removed steps and run into the ice radar antennae.

On 14 October we stopped for fuel at the depot we had laid at the end of the autumn traverse line. The further south we went the more the weather improved as we escaped the influence of the pressure systems which generally move along the coast. On a nice day the sunshine melted the frost on the 'dozer windows. I looked out on the infinite, gradually undulating white landscape, its surface textured by the irregular sastrugi that continually changed form with the constant abrading of the wind-driven snow grains. The scene was right in front of me, yet I felt separated from it and thought it was like looking into an aquarium. The realisation gradually dawned that I was the one in the aquarium, the artificial world with the specially controlled climate, and was looking through the glass at the real world outside.

Along the route we continued the glaciological work, and measurements using the satellite survey equipment were taken at twenty ice movement stations during the traverse. Often, while one party was at a station, the other would go onto the next and collect data there, so at times we were around fifty kilometres apart.

When travelling, we usually got up between 6.00 and 6.30 am and Brian started the vehicles and checked the generator. After breakfast I turned on the ice radar and made sure it and the manual logging sheets were ready. The 'dozers were

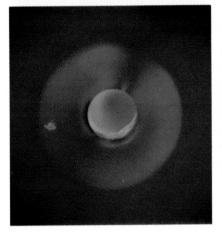

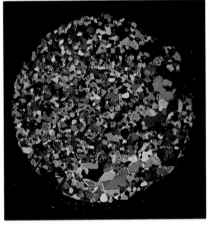

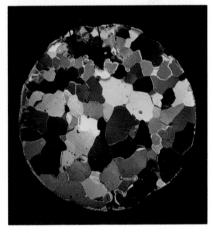

Top: Andy Wood drilling, Rik Thwaites measuring and Qin Dahe sectioning ice cores
Above: Looking down a drill hole. Core sections from eleven and eighteen metres under polarised light

hooked up and the living van taken alongside the nearest cane. Jim would take a sun shot, zero the odometer and record information such as position, time, temperature, barometric pressure and ice depth. He then looked for the next cane using the navigation radar and we would leave by 7.30 or 8.00 am. Along the way we stopped at each cane to make the snow accumulation measurements.

The highlights from my diary of the day's journey for 17 October read:

Up at 6.30 am and after some odd jobs we left the others at 9.20 am and headed off for our next station at GC39. Today they are drilling a thirty metre ice core hole.

For most of the day there were showers of tiny ice crystals flying and glittering in the air which created a bright halo around the sun with a parhelion (a mock sun) on either side. Later in the afternoon the sky cleared completely and the temperature fell. When we left this morning it was – 32.8 °C and warmed to a

maximum of – 27.6 °C at 1.17 pm. From there the temperatures dropped: – 30 °C at 4.00 pm, – 45 °C at 8.54 pm and – 51.2 °C at 10.24 pm when we stopped.

We covered thirty-five kilometres today and on arriving set up the satellite survey gear. After doing this, refuelling the 'dozers and parking the vans it was 12.45 am. We cooked tea, washed up, filled the snow melter and now it is 2.30 am and Jim and Brian have gone to bed.

I was outside a few minutes ago where the temperature is – 55.8 °C and noticed I could hear my breath freeze! When I breathed out, the moisture sud-denly froze, making a faint but

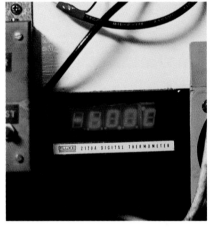

distinct hissing, crackling sound. I was really surprised!

It is quite light in the southern sky and I found this strange when I walked outside expecting it to be dark. Tonight the sun set at 8.30 pm, but because of an inversion a mirage of part of the sun lay as a bar of yellow-orange light on the horizon for the next forty-five minutes.

The following evening, the others caught up with us and that night we had the coldest temperature of the trip. After midnight the temperature fell to −60 °C and I went outside to see what it was like. 'It was just cold,' I noted, 'nothing special.' Later, Russell woke and saw the thermometer in his van reading −64 °C. It was quite warm in bed, though, and I felt glad I was not in a tent. Inside *Gordon* we ran an electric blower heater on low in the cold-porch plus another inside with a thermostat to keep the temperature around +16 °C. Much higher and it felt too warm. My bunk was the

lowest and I kept my electric blanket on the floor under the mattress and ran it during the day to keep the bedding dry from condensation. I rarely had it on at night as it got too hot and I wore summer pyjamas with a doona for covering.

The cold affected things outside, though. When we had begun to experience temperatures in the minus forties, *Gordon*'s navigation radar antenna had frozen up again much to my dismay. With limited resources for repairs, I took the heat-trace element from our spare sink drainpipe warmer and wrapped it around

the neck of the antenna housing where the bearings were. Covered with a layer of blanket and aluminium foil to keep out the wind, this make-shift heater saw out the traverse. The low temperatures also played havoc with the paint-work on the generator vans. Their sides turned silver as paint literally peeled off over-night with the contraction of the metal, leaving a line of orange flakes on the snow in the morning.

Working late one night I was interrupted at 2.00 am by the generator stopping. The power fail alarm saved me waking Brian who went and started the small emergency generator. Its limited output restricted the use of heaters and, because I was starting to feel cold, I thought I would light the gas stove. It was so cold, though, that the regulator on the bottle outside had frozen, cutting off the gas. Meanwhile, Brian had troubles of his own. The generator had stopped because the fuel in the line from the tank had begun to jell, becoming so thick that it

would not flow. He spent till morning replumbing the fuel line to a drum of ATK he put inside the van and ran the generator from this at night.

Warmer climates sometimes came to mind and on one occasion we sat around the kitchen table listening to Russell talk about the Northern Territory and tropical areas he had worked in. I then opened a present marked 'When you feel like a change of scenery' which contained a picture book of Australia and it was a refreshing reminder to us of what trees, rocks, warmth and bodies of unfrozen water are like.

The temperatures back at Casey were more conducive to outside exercise than ours, and on one of the nightly radio skeds we heard about a lively excursion the doctor had been on. Bruce had been out walking on the thirteen-centimetre-thick sea ice when, without warning, a leopard seal smashed up through the ice from behind and latched onto his rear end!

Swimming underneath, the seal would have been able to see his shape moving above and presumably thought he was a penguin. The surprised seal, though I doubt as shocked as Bruce, let go and slipped back into the water without its quarry, which it would have been capable of dragging under. Bruce's legacy was some teeth punctures — he claimed they did not require stitches, though we suspected this was because someone else would have to put them in — and a pair of holed trousers. These he wanted to show his grandchildren and declined the offer to

have them put in a glass case alongside the stuffed leopard seal at head office.

The next AWS site, GC41, at 71° 36.2′ S, 111° 15.1′ E was reached on 24 October and the following day we erected the mast in a ten knot (19 km/h), −47°C breeze. It was colder, but the conditions were more pleasant than when we had put up the first weather station. Testing the two good sets of AWS electronics had shown up defects in their wind measurement circuits and, although I fixed a design error at this stop, we left with a fault in the wind peak circuit remaining a mystery.

Far inland while ascending a long, windswept rise we were amazed to discover the tracks from the previous traverse which had gone that way in 1979. The slippery surface was hard and glazed and shone in the sun. The tracks appeared for another two kilometres before the slope eased and became snow-covered again. That night, 8 November, the sun did not fully set, only partially going behind the horizon

before rising again. Continuous sunshine was to be with us for some time.

Brian, Jim and I joined the *Flash* team at 'The Crossroads' on 12 November. Here at GM13 our traverse line crossed the Russian one which ran from Mirny roughly south-east to a point called Dome C. Their last traverse had travelled the route between December 1983 and February 1984 and Trevor Hamley, an Australian glaciologist whom we had worked with before leaving Australia, had been with them. The Russians had left a present for us which contained mostly foodstuffs and the inevitable bottle of Vodka which was frozen solid. There was also a letter from them which read:

To: Australian Traverse Team 1984

From: Soviet (Mirny — Dome C) Traverse Team 1983-1984

Dear Colleagues!

In the Antarctic inland there are [sic] not anything except the endless white desert. In this place the traverses cross has [sic] a big symbolic meaning — it is a point of meeting, friendship and peace.

Accept our small gift, please, as a symbol of friendship between Australian and Soviet peoples.

For the peaceful world, without wars!

It was signed by their team leader and members. On our way home we reciprocated with a letter and gifts to their next traverse team to come through.

From The Crossroads, the *Gordon* party detoured along the Russian line to do an ice movement station and later caught up again with *Flash*. We had depoted my 'dozer, *Wendy*, farther back and I now worked on the AWS problems while travelling in *Gordon*. Two days before reaching the end of our line I diagnosed the fault with the wind peak circuit. It had been made exactly according to the circuit diagram — which had been drawn incorrectly.

Our farthest south was reached on 19 November at GC46, 74° 8.3′ S, 109° 49.7′ E, elevation 3,073 metres. Approaching this spot I had measured the ice to be over four kilometres thick. The position is not that far south considering that Amundsen and Scott started their trips to the South Pole from around 78° S. We were still 1,763 kilometres from the Pole, but had begun outside the Antarctic Circle and were 873 kilometres south of Casey's latitude of 66° 17′ S.

The satellite survey equipment was set up and the following morning the last, and finally debugged, weather station was erected and switched on. This time the weather was pleasant, with the temperature in the minus thirties and only a few knots of wind, so there was no need to keep running inside to warm up.

The next couple of days saw various activities such as Rik working in a pit taking snow samples for later analysis and examining the yearly layers for their type, hardness and density. Brian erected a monolithic drum beacon and we celebrated reaching the end of our line plus my birthday with a barbecue lunch and a roast dinner that 'night'. Amongst the presents and cards which had been brought for me there was a prophetic letter from my brother written 'from a distance of eleven months ago' in which he said, 'I hope that everything has been as you would like this year — not necessarily easy, but satisfying.' A nice gift was to receive a telex from head office which read in part: 'Data is one hundred per cent okay. Wind peak and mean are good...

Top and centre left: The Russian present
Opposite, above and right: Erecting a weather station

Time to do U-turn and head towards equator.'

With some leisure for a change, I decided it was time to wash the sheet on my bed, but quickly discovered it was not going to be easy. Around the bottom bunk there was little air circulation and moisture had condensed on the wall, frozen and built up a thick ice layer. This had enveloped the sheet at the side and end of the mattress, though in bed it was still warm and dry. The sheet was so firmly iced to the wall that my determined efforts to pull it free were useless and the only way I could remove it was by using a hammer and cold chisel!

Rik, Andy and Russell headed north on 23 November and we followed the next day. On the way home there was less work to be done, but Rik had to take temperature measurements in bore holes drilled on our way inland and we had a meteorological program to carry out. This entailed a balloon flight, morning and evening if possible, visually tracking the balloon with a theodolite to determine wind speed with elevation and receiving temperature, pressure and relative humidity data from a radiosonde the balloon carried. These flights had been attempted on the way out, but the cold weather had made them difficult. We had stopped them after a flight when the theodolite froze solid and, while filling the balloon, the rubber hose between it and the gas bottle, as Rik put it, 'snapped like a twig'.

The weather became poorer and the temperature rose as we migrated north and I wondered how $-30\,°C$ ever felt cold! A sunny day required the heater to be off in the 'dozer and, as we experienced the hotter twenties, teens and single figure negative temperatures, I left the door or roof hatch open for fresh air. However, my brother knew real heat. He sent me a telex asking if I would like to swap places with him in western Queensland where he'd had temperatures up to $+50\,°C$!

While over 300 kilometres from the nearest coastline, Russell spotted the first life we had seen in nearly three months other than ourselves when three snow petrels suddenly appeared and flew around his 'dozer. After Rik and Andy saw them too, he was convinced he was not hallucinating.

The two parties separated, *Flash* going off to do more ice movement stations on another line while *Gordon* went back to the first AWS at A028 so I could get it going. It still would not work properly and I spent a frustrating week trying to find why the data was correct when I tested the circuitry, but was scrambled when received from the satellites. My hopes rose when a data test pattern was sent and received perfectly and I reconnected the sensors. The final word came from Australia — still bad. The telex contained a quote that was like an epilogue: 'never underestimate the inane perversity of inanimate objects'. It seemed that the transmitter was faulty and so we decided to take the electronics back to Casey for repair and have the following year's traverse team bring it back. I was disappointed not to have

Left: Preparing a met balloon
Above: Ground drift at 2.00 am

three out of three stations working, but felt glad the project was over and thanked God for my many answered prayers during it!

I was pleased to leave A028 behind on 19 December and four days later we met up with the others again and crossed The Trench before camping. The next day, Christmas Eve, we were welcomed at the centre of Law Dome by a party of six from Casey. I was surprised how much I enjoyed seeing and talking with new people. They brought fresh fruit, vegetables, eggs and two large presents which contained a deck chair and a Christmas tree. More important was our mail which had come off *Nella Dan* after she reached the ice edge north of Casey on 13 November. Christmas day was spent opening presents, socialising and eating roast turkey for dinner with twelve people crammed into *Flash*. Our visitors set off on 27 December, leaving us to carry out an ice

radar survey around the summit area of Law Dome in preparation for a future ice core drilling program.

We saw in the new year, 1985, sitting around a fire on the snow with the sun near the horizon and glowing pale yellow through an ice fog. Two days later, while waiting out some bad weather, I wrote the following reflections on the traverse in my diary:

Casey is four to six days away. I know I will be there soon and everything will be different, but after spending three-and-a-half months in this van with never anything but the vast, white plateau to view, it seems the norm and if we spent another three months out here it would continue to be the accepted way of life. The plateau certainly has 'a magic of its own' as Peter Keage, the 1976 glaciologist, told me back at Kingston, but the times when I was able to relax and enjoy its grandeur were too few.

I'm sure that looking back on traverse I will remember it as a great time, but it has mostly been hard work for us. I read about old sledging journeys and

romanticise about them, particularly the epic ones like Mawson's, Amundsen's and Scott's, but these were a combination of arduous work, great discomfort, danger and sometimes horror — certainly not trips to be envied. However, once accomplished we can look back with great satisfaction at problems, challenges, difficulties and hardships overcome. Of course the hardships encountered these days are far fewer than those of the 'heroic' or, to quote Laseron, 'old style' age, as we travel in comparative luxury — but there are still some. For us there are new dangers arising from the modern methods of travel and accommodation.

There is now a lot more scientific work that can be, and is carried out, but the weather is the same and stops us like it stopped the manhaulers.

Four days into the new year and we were on the final stretch home. *Icebird*, a new ship on her maiden voyage, had arrived at Casey on 30 December and the two helicopters from her flew out to us with some jolliers for a brief visit. That night I saw the sun set for the first time in nearly two

Left: Andy Wood looking up the shaft in S2
Above: Ice crystals from S2

months and we camped by an old American glaciological site called S2.

S2 had been established for the International Geophysical Year and its main feature is a hand-dug, thirty-five-metre-deep shaft in which the bottom snow layers date back to approximately 1783. To reach the shaft required a descent through a trap door and down a ladder about ten metres to a tunnel system, the main one connecting the top of the shaft to a canvas Jamesway hut. The tunnels were originally trenches in the surface with sheets of plywood placed over them, but

along with the hut were now buried under the years of snow accumulation since 1957. The hut was half crushed and, in the sides of the shaft, once circular ice core holes were distorted into weird shapes as the snow slowly compressed to ice under its own weight.

The next evening we drove through Lanyon Junction around 9.30 pm and continued down towards Casey. Two Hagglunds came up to meet us and, parking the traverse trains, we were rushed the last kilometres home over melting snow which would have bogged the dozers. *Icebird* was to sail

that night and some of the 1984 winterers would be leaving, so it was a last chance of farewelling them. We reached Casey to find a barbecue in progress outside the kitchen. Afterwards I recorded my impressions of our arrival in my diary:

There were cheers from the '84 guys with much backslapping and handshaking. A beaut welcome and it was great to be back. I felt extremely happy. I told people that it had been good on traverse, but I was glad to be back — and that's how we all felt.

7
Summer excursions

I DID NOT BOTHER SETTING an alarm clock for the first few days after arriving back at Casey. The small luxuries of civilisation were a joy: I could control the temperature of the water when I showered and there was no snowmelter to fill afterwards; automatic washing machines replaced a bucket; and the buildings had a wonderful feeling of spacious-

Below: Met radar dome at Casey

ness. I could pass someone in the corridor without each of us having to turn sideways.

The station was a different place to what I had left nearly four months previously. I had been able to walk outside onto a road of snow, whereas now there was a two metre drop from the landings to a dusty track continuously used by trucks, Hagglunds and trikes. The Casey rebuilding program was in full swing and the

majority of people were builders there for the summer. The 1985 traverse team had arrived and they began to prepare the vans for the autumn traverse as soon as we moved our gear out.

The six of us who had been on traverse were given a break for a rest. We each were to spend a week in turn assisting a Dutch ornithologist, Jan van Franeker, who was studying birds on an island.

On 13 January Jan and I set out in an inflatable boat and motored off for Ardery Island. We wore rubber immersion suits over our clothes which would keep us dry and warm if we fell in. The sea temperature was around 0 °C (sea water freezes at approximately − 2 °C) and, unprotected, a person may die within minutes if left in the water. Later I could not resist trying out the suit. I slid into the sea and lay on my back.

'This is weird!' I exclaimed. 'I feel like I'm on top of the water I'm so buoyant. Floating on the Dead Sea must be like this — only warmer!'

On our way to the island we passed the Adelie penguin rookery on Shirley Island. Groups of fat chicks with insatiable appetites stood along the rocky shore waiting for parent birds to return with more food. The water was busy with black and white torpedoes swimming below the smooth surface and occasionally porpoising for a quick breath. They shot into the air, still enveloped in a glistening sheath of icy water, plopped cleanly

back into the dark sea and swam on, the whole exercise done in one effortless movement.

The penguins and the Weddell seals lolling on ice flows were happily living in an environment potentially fatal to us and our movements were tracked by a helicopter flying overhead in case we ran into trouble. We had to travel by boat because helicopters are not allowed to land on Ardery Island. It lies in a Specially Protected Area, one of a number nominated by the consultative members of the Antarctic Treaty. A permit must be obtained to enter these areas and flying a helicopter too close could be detrimental to the bird colonies.

Jan guided the boat through a band of pack ice and I looked across at the island. It was a little over one kilometre long and steep-sided. We landed at its western end at Mast Point, hauled the boat well above the water line and tied it down tightly before carrying our supplies up to the hut. This looked like a big red apple with portholes and I sat

cosily in it that evening gazing at the view. Three kilometres away over the ruffled blue water, the ice cliffs of the mainland glowed in the sun, and the hills, moraines and snow slopes took on a pinkish hue. The cables securing the hut hummed in the wind, a few metres away the grey-brown rock dropped down to the sea thirty metres below and the air was filled with gliding, wheeling and flapping birds.

Joining Jan on his rounds on the following days I learnt that southern (or Antarctic) fulmars, Antarctic petrels, snow petrels, Cape pigeons (more correctly Cape petrels), Wilson's storm petrels and south polar skuas were breeding on the island. He was studying the first four, with emphasis on the fulmars. The birds nested around the island's sides on the bare rock or under boulders with only the skuas inhabiting the flatter top of the island. Different species had different nesting habits and

Top left: Jan van Franeker
Centre left: Testing an exposure suit
Bottom left: Adelie chick being fed

Above: Jan weighing a snow petrel
Left: Antarctic petrel and chick

generally congregated in separate areas, although some mixing did occur.

Jan had marked out certain rookery areas for investigation and comparison and he made twice-daily checks of some of these. In study areas nests were given an identifying number and the nesting pair banded. My job was to help catch birds and then act as scribe while Jan banded them and took measurements such as their wing, head and bill length, weight and number of tail and flight feathers. To keep a bird confined while taking these statistics, it was placed in a closely-fitting, tapered cloth bag open at both ends. The bird's head came out the small opening and the bag kept it from flapping its wings and hurting itself. Most species flew away immediately they were released, but the Antarctic petrels had a curious habit of sitting on the ground for a short time, seemingly composing themselves before taking off.

I have never tired of the delight of being able to approach Antarctic wildlife closely before they show signs of being uncomfortable with a human presence. Some penguins have been so curious of me that they have come within reach to examine me, while seals generally choose to ignore people after taking a brief look. This lack of fear is due to their having few or no enemies on land and it has an Eden-like quality about it.

In places the nesting birds dotted the ground making us careful where we trod. Because they were dedicated to their eggs and chicks they hardly moved and were easily caught by hand. The fulmars and the Antarctic petrels were the most docile, but the Cape pigeons and snow petrels often spat some of their stomach contents as a defence. Used against another bird, like a marauding skua, the oily substance takes away the waterproofness of the feathers.

Left: Antarctic fulmars, Ardery Island
Above: Jan inside the hut
Right: A Weddell seal

When the bird lands on the sea, its body can get wet and its feathers sodden so that it may not be able to take off again, or it could die later from cold or pneumonia. The characteristic of the spit which affects humans is its aroma: it stinks! I had first-hand experience of this when my hat blew in front of a Cape pigeon and the startled bird immediately jettisoned its last meal onto it.

The skuas were by far the most aggressive birds and would fly at us from behind screeching and try to kick our heads. They laid their eggs on the ground by a large rock and,

when hatched, the chicks would wander about in proximity to the 'nest'. I knew I was approaching a nest area when I was swooped on by an adult bird plus the site would be littered with bits of other birds' chicks and eggs on which the skuas fed.

After a day of bad weather that had restricted us to brief trips outside, I went for a stroll when the wind died away. In the eerie stillness of the midnight quiet, I walked from the hut and all sounds came clearly through the darkness. My footsteps echoed crisply from the cliff opposite and hard pellets

Top: Cape pigeon and chick
Above: An abandoned egg is taken by a hungry skua

of sago snow fell hissing on the rock. I stopped to listen — a bird flew overhead, its feathers rustling as it flapped its wings. The sea slapped gently against the shore and from faraway in the north came a rushing noise as breezes there roughened the water. A distant, thunderous booming abruptly drowned everything and signalled the birth of a new iceberg as it was calved from the floating snout of the Vanderford Glacier, fifteen kilometres away.

I was sad to leave Ardery Island. A stark place, it was attractive to me for its sights and sounds and a warmth of feeling from the impressive birds rearing their young.

Back at crowded and noisy Casey I documented work from traverse and ran and upgraded the upper atmosphere physics (UAP) experiments. In the long, summer evenings after work or on Sundays many of us went walking, skiing or driving from the station.

On a skiing trip to O'Brien Bay, I noticed a leopard seal sleeping on the edge of the sea ice. A group of frightened

Adelie penguins were standing nearby, nervously looking between the seal and the water. They know the difference between a leopard seal and a harmless Weddell or crabeater. On land, the leopard poses little threat to them because they can easily avoid it, but their lives are at stake if they enter the water and it follows them. Frustrated, one individual decided to take the risk and waddled along the edge away from the seal and dived in. The others watched the leopard's reaction and when it continued to snooze they followed, swimming off at a great rate.

Top: Antarctic fulmars doing head-sweeping movements
Above left: Skuas in an aggression display
Above: A snow petrel in flight

I decided to have a closer look at the seal. Once down on the melting ice I took my skis off, but carried one stock to test the ice. It required a snakes and ladders path around cracks and melt pools to reach the seal which only seemed interested in sleeping and showed its mouth full of rather impressive teeth when it yawned. I kept a respectful distance. Becoming weary of being photographed, it took to the water and then

made me uneasy by poking its head out, resting its chin on the edge of the ice close by and staring at me before diving under the ice. I had visions of it bursting up from below and grabbing me as had happened to Bruce, so I smartly retreated to the closest piece of thick ice. I waited anxiously until the seal emerged and hauled itself out of the water, thirty metres away. This relieved me but terrorised an Adelie which had been standing at that spot. Squawking and flapping, it fled while the leopard seal settled back to sleep.

A bird which did not survive a life-threatening situation as that Adelie penguin had was a skua named Oscar. Skuas often congregated around the kitchen for food scraps and this one in particular spent most of its time there and had become very unafraid of people, hardly moving out of the way for them. Oscar apparently was not good at discerning the difference between people and vehicles. One of the carpenters was charged with 'skua-slaughter' after running over 'beloved Oscar', though he claimed Oscar was jaywalking. The next day this poem anonymously appeared on the noticeboard in the mess:

Ode to Oscar (Beloved)

Oscar, dear Oscar, we'll all miss
    your cry,
As you'd screech and you'd
    scream for more apple pie.
Your little brown body would
    waddle and sway,
After gutsing our garbage you'd
    not fly away.

One day on the roadway you
    patiently sat,
When up drove a chippie as
    blind as a bat.
'Twas carefree Abbo driving the
    ute,
And with a squish and a squawk
    you'd had the boot.

Now you don't look the same
    with tracks down your back,
As our garbage disposal you've
    had the sack.
We think you're a wimp to just
    get up and die,
But Oscar, dear Oscar, we'll all
    miss your cry!

As the arrival date for the last ship of the season approached, I spent a lot of time packing cartons of UAP chart records, equipment and personal gear. *Icebird* arrived on 13 March and at this late stage the faulty AWS remained defective despite my having replaced the trans-

mitter with a new one from Australia. Both those at head office and myself were out of ideas as to what could be wrong and I had asked Evan Davis, an engineer at Casey for the summer, if he would examine the problem. His investigation led to the discovery that the electronics appeared to work perfectly in its test mode, but not when run normally. This was confirmed on 15 March, the day I was to sail, and with no time for further checking I left the drum with my replacement, Ross Walsh, to set up at A028. It would be running in its test mode, which meant that its data was less reliable but still usable.

After a day of hurried last-minute arrangements, I boarded a LARC for the ship. We had the usual type of sendoff from the new crew — plenty of flour bombs and water. Wearing garbage bags for protection was of little help when the LARC was driven under the bucket of a front-end loader which tipped its contents of sea water, drenching us!

At 9.30 pm I walked to *Icebird*'s stern and watched the lights of Casey fade. It had been a busy year and, after rushing all day, I still had to come to terms with the fact that I had left and could relax.

The next morning I was disappointed to find that we had passed through most of the pack ice during the night. The ship had to call at Macquarie Island on its way to Hobart and I looked forward to this as we travelled on in grey weather, with little interesting scenery except for a few birds following the ship. The only work I had to do was assist with a couple of meteorological balloon flights. People passed the time by watching videos, talking, standing around on the bridge, eating, sleeping and counting the days to Hobart.

The ocean was rough at times and I found it difficult to sleep while the sea did its best to pitch me from the top bunk onto the floor. In a confused sea one night the ship rolled to an angle of 45°, freeing cans of drink and gear which then clattered madly about the cabin. Qin Dahe attempted to re-stow things while I clung to the bed and tried to prevent myself joining the havoc of debris on the floor.

Within a day's sailing of Macquarie Island the ship was given an escort by giant petrels and a wandering albatross. Early in the morning of 23 March, we sailed up the east side of the island and dropped anchor. Everyone had been called at 4.30 am and, when I first saw the island, I was momentarily startled — it was all green, even though I knew it would be. It looked so different from what I had seen for the past year.

We were ashore on the LARCs at 6.00 am and I soon set off on one of the short tours that had been arranged for us. I left with a group which walked down to the Nuggets and during the hour it took us to stroll there the sun began to break through the heavy, grey cloud and added life to the splendid scenery about us. On the beach which curved south from Nuggets Point were groups of king penguins and a large crowd of moulting royal penguins with more royals swimming to and from the sea through the surf. Above the beach sat the rusting remains of the digesters and steam boilers which had once rendered oil from penguins and elephant seals. The bottoms of old barrels, which may have been for holding recovered oil, were embedded in the dirt as well as the base of the sealers' old works building.

Above and right: Royal penguins on Macquarie Island

I knelt on the sand and was soon surrounded by a group of superbly coloured king penguins. Shorter and more slender than the emperor, they are equally inquisitive, and one tugged gently at my finger when I held it out.

The royal penguins use Nuggets Creek as a pathway to their rookeries upstream and travel along it in groups for safety. As I walked up the creek, I disturbed a giant petrel eating a piece of a penguin and farther upstream two skuas were pecking at the remains of a head. After ten minutes' walking I suddenly faced tens of thousands of royals — a stunning, black and white, wall-to-wall carpet of penguins hemmed in by the green tussock grass.

While I took in this extreme example of 'birds of a feather', a group of them gathered at the creek entrance until their number was large enough for them to instil confidence in one another to venture to the beach. These royal penguins only had to face natural enemies. The threat from mankind was removed when the Tasmanian government decided to stop issuing licences to the oil industry in 1919. However, the sealers introduced cats, rabbits, rats, mice and the flightless weka which continue to interfere with the original ecosystem.

Back on the beach we encountered some of the local skuas. These birds, brown skuas, are darker and braver than the south polar skua of Antarctica. One of them stole a blower brush from my camera bag and flew off with it while another concentrated on dragging away a jumper. I was told that they will thieve food from the kitchen if given the opportunity.

Above: King penguins and Qin Dahe
Left and right: Elephant seals

life and beauty to be savoured on this unusual continent which could easily be damaged or destroyed by exploitation. It is essential that the countries of the world agree to use the area solely for research and tourism. Mankind's greed, our unwillingness to share equally and our failure to learn from the errors of the past do not bode well for an untouched Antarctica, though.

Although not able to see everything I had hoped to by the time the LARCs returned us to *Icebird*, I was content with my experiences: and the weather had been sunny most of the time. Rain or mist usually occurs on over three hundred days a year at Macquarie Island and by that evening its top was enveloped in cloud.

Interesting animal stories abound on Macquarie Island — like the artistic elephant seal that wriggled across a porch after knocking over some open paint tins, or the time a weka stopped a botanical experiment by running off with a rubber bulb.

Back at the ANARE station, I climbed Wireless Hill. This hill derived its name from the radio masts set up on it by Douglas Mawson at the start of his 1911-14 expedition. The party of five he left on the island were to relay messages between his Antarctic base and Australia, report their local weather observations, survey Macquarie Island for mapping and study its wildlife and geology. It was Mawson who later canvassed to have Macquarie Island declared a wildlife sanctuary — which it was in May 1933.

In the Macquarie Island Nature Reserve all native flora and fauna is now protected and similarly many people promote the idea of making Antarctica a world park. I find this proposition appealing as there is much

Above: *Icebird* sailing up
the River Derwent into Hobart

The helicopters from *Icebird* had been busy resupplying field huts on the island, but with the job unfinished they had to fly again the next morning. The weather was bad but the pilots flew, following the coastline to avoid getting lost in the thick cloud capping the island. I spent my time watching king and gentoo penguins swim about the ship and threw pieces of bread to giant petrels that floated about like ducks. They spread their wings and literally ran across the surface of the water to reach the prize first. In the early afternoon the work was finished and the helicopters and LARCs, were stowed.

At 4.00 pm *Icebird* sailed for Hobart, full of weary expeditioners impatient to be home.

During the morning of 27 March, Tasmania came in sight and we sailed up the Derwent River in sunny weather. On the dock were families and friends eager to greet us and joyful were the many reunions. When one of the crew used a ship's crane to off-load some of our large and heavy boxes, the wharfies complained. The gear had to be swung aboard again and then manhandled back onto the dock. This experience brought home to me with a jolt that I was back in 'civilisation'!

8
Nella Dan beset

NAUSEA IS MISERY. *Nella Dan* was off the Tasmanian coast gyrating in a swell and I felt ill. Would I cope with the conditions we expected in the coming weeks, sailing across the stormy Southern Ocean to Heard Island? This was a one-day voyage out of Hobart, a trial cruise to give scientists and engineers a chance to install and check the operation of equipment for the marine science cruise. After the ship returned to port, I enjoyed one last night ashore, sleeping in a bed which did not rock about and eating at a level table.

On 16 September 1985, one year and a day after setting out on the 1984 Casey spring traverse, I sailed on an eventful voyage titled ADBEX (Antarctic Division BIOMASS Experiment) III to Heard Island and Antarctica. Various biological and glaciological programs were planned, most of the action beginning after we had left a party on Heard Island.

I quickly gained my sea legs and survived the dirty weather the roaring forties and furious fifties hurled at us. Although not as bad as some had feared, it was quite enough for those with sensitive stomachs. In our worst storm I braced myself on the bridge and, from behind the protection of the spray-lashed windows, took in the wild scene outside. Heavy black clouds pressed down from the sky and the fierce, boisterous wind pushed along waves up to ten metres high, the white froth

of their breaking crests being swept away horizontally by the gale. *Nella* literally shuddered sometimes as she plunged head-long into a wave, sending a deluge of water bursting upwards from her bow.

I made my way to the trawl deck below the helideck where the view was both spectacular and wet. As the ship rode over another wave with its stern still high on the passing crest, a deep, watery valley sloped away behind. *Nella* slid down the back of the wave before the bow rose with the next oncoming hill of water, pushing down the stern which occasionally sank so deep that the sea's surface was level with the helideck. Caught standing on the trawl deck when this happened, I found my view obliterated and replaced by a solid wall of dark water which instantly cascaded over the bulwarks. I dived and lay spreadeagled atop a canvas-covered winch as the water foamed about the deck. Exhilarating it might have been, but after the water drained away I beat a hasty retreat to a

safer spot before the next wave.

In calmer conditions we launched three drifting buoys which transmitted data on weather conditions and the ocean currents to satellites. We also searched for two others whose batteries were near the end of their lives. The position of the second was in the pack ice and, being painted white, was not particularly easy to see. The promise of a bottle of an alcoholic beverage of the spotter's choice failed to improve eyesight and, with limited time, we changed course for Heard Island.

Nella Dan reached this lone, glacier-capped volcanic island on Sunday 29 September. The island is twenty to twenty-five kilometres in diameter and is principally one mountain, the active volcano Big Ben, which towers some 2,800 metres above the sea. As we sailed along its south-western coast-line, cloud shrouded all but the lower slopes and steam bil-lowed from the vicinity of the

Gotley Glacier on its side. When we rounded Mt Dixon on the Laurens Peninsula, everyone was surprised to see *Icebird* on her way to Hobart for the season and carrying tourists. Unable to land anyone, *Icebird* continued on her journey soon after our meeting.

It was too late in the day to begin unloading operations at Atlas Cove, so *Nella Dan* sailed up and down in the lee of the island. Snowstorms inter-

mittently veiled the island. Between these, ethereal light played through towering, wind-torn clouds, spotlighting the crevassed, crumbling slopes of the glaciers on Big Ben. Giant petrels and flocks of Cape pigeons wheeled about the ship, a suitable finishing touch to an awe-inspiring scene.

We were prevented from going ashore on Monday by strong winds and fierce squalls with low cloud and rain

Above: Approaching Heard Island
Right: Glacier-covered slopes of Big Ben

throughout the morning and snow and hail in the afternoon. That night the cloud lifted and the bright moon lit up snow-covered Big Ben. Steam rose in clouds from the summit, glowing orange-red from molten lava beneath.

Heard Island's first human inhabitants were sealers who began exploiting the animal life in the 1850s. ANARE parties had wintered from 1948 to 1954 but in the following thirty-odd years there had been little activity. A few summer operations had been conducted, a United States group wintered in 1969 and three private expeditions had stayed briefly. The first of these, 'The South Indian Ocean Expedition to Heard Island, 1964-65', sailed to Heard Island in the schooner *Patanela* and climbed Big Ben for the first time. In 1983 this ascent was repeated by the 'Heard Island Expedition' and the 'Heard Island DX Association' expedition also visited in

Above: The old ANARE station on Heard Island
Right: Jocelyne Hughes, biologist, and Lynn Williams, medical officer, cleaning out a hut

113

the old steam powered whale-
chaser *Cheynes II*. Sjoerd
Jongens, one of the three
people with whom I shared
Cabin 8 on this cruise, had
been on *Cheynes II* and told us
about his adventures, including
the trip home to Albany in
Western Australia when they
travelled 1,580 kilometres
under improvised sail because
of a fuel shortage.

The purpose of our visit to
Heard Island was to re-establish
the scientific station at Atlas
Cove. Since the site now had
historical significance, we were
required to record its status on
our arrival. I was fortunate in
being given the task of pho-
tographing it before the shore
party moved in. The weather
had taken a severe toll on the
old buildings and they were in
a poor state. I spent my time
ashore helping shovel and
sweep black sand and dirt from
the most habitable huts before
returning to the ship on a LARC
in driving snow.

Above: The helicopters are readied for flying
Right: A derelict hut at the old ANARE station

By Wednesday afternoon the Atlas Cove camp was set up and then bad weather hampered our operations. It was not until Friday evening that a four-man party had been landed at Spit Bay, the LARCs dropped off at the main base, and we could sail for the pack ice. If all went according to plan, we would be back at the end of the month to carry out further work on the island and in the surrounding ocean and visit the French station of Port-aux-Français on Kerguelen Island before leaving with everyone for Hobart.

Nella reached the pack ice on 7 October and we began our principal project, that of making an estimate of the population of crabeater seals and their breeding biology. This was under the direction of our expedition leader, Dr Knowles Kerry. The seals were not found along the outer margin of the pack where they were expected and we headed south in our search for them.

Above: *Nella Dan* and LARCs in Atlas Cove
Left: Pancake ice

As our experienced captain, Arne Sørensen, piloted *Nella Dan* through the pack ice, the glaciologists, Joe Jacka and Rik Thwaites, noted the changing ice forms. To me the most obvious and interesting variations came in the early stages. Firstly, the waves became smoothed to a rounded, rolling swell as if covered with oil when we encountered grease ice — small spicules of ice floating on the surface. This gave way to a covering of spongy white lumps a few centimetres across called shuga ice that further damped the waves. Later, the ship was surrounded as far as the eye could see by pancake ice which lay like lily pads smothering the water, their perimeters edged with a thin ice wall from jostling each other. Small at first, the cakes grew to be a couple of metres across as we proceeded. Broken pieces of first-year ice then slowed our progress until we met with large continuous floes which had to be negotiated. Captain Sørensen often climbed into the crow's-nest and steered the ship from there, picking a route through narrow leads and areas of open water called polynyi.

Wildlife became more

Above and right: *Nella Dan* stopped in pack ice at night
Below: Pushing through the pack at night

abundant with Adelie penguins, emperor penguins and killer whales being sighted but, despite aerial surveys, the crabeater seals remained elusive, only one being seen. The chief steward, Ruben Nielsen, had a gibe at us when he put 'mock seal' on the menu and later another crew member left a pair of what he called 'special crabeater binoculars' on the bridge: two wine bottles and a drawing of a seal in each eyepiece!

On 20 October we were all shaken when Kim Nielsen died after an accident. Kim, one of our cooks, had slipped and fallen down the steep steps of the galley and hit his head severely. A spirit of comrade-ship had developed between passengers and crew while working together and after this tragedy a subdued atmosphere came over the ship.

The coast of Enderby Land on the Antarctic continent came in sight on 27 October and Knowles Kerry and Paul Ensor were flown across to Mount Biscoe to complete the line of study between the edge of the pack ice and land. When they were back on board, *Nella* turned and started the journey for Heard Island.

It was then that the pack ice through which we had sailed that morning began to close about the ship as it was pushed along by a strengthening easterly wind. Within a few hours, *Nella Dan* was immobile and there was no water visible between the compacted and jumbled floes. Pressure ridges several metres high formed shattered lines across the land-scape as floes piled up like packs of cards forced together, leaving large slabs slanting down under the water. The bow of the ship lifted as ice was driven beneath. We were stuck fast.

Right: Thick conditions on the *Nella Dan*

It was ironic that at this time helicopter reconnaissance revealed the presence of the crabeater seals we had come so far to find! Over the next few days the broken ice surrounding us froze together forming one huge piece and, although locked solid, *Nella* was in no danger. The threat of being crushed occurs when a ship is caught between large, moving floes.

We were all hoping and expecting the ice to crack up shortly so that we could be on our way, but made the most of the time by continuing the scientific programs. Once the ice was cemented together we could leave the ship and walk about, which was useful for both work and recreation. The glaciologists had ample opportunities for checking sea ice movements and taking core samples while the divers filmed and studied krill behaviour on the underside of the ice. Some projects were modified to suit the heavy ice conditions.

Some sports-minded individuals set up a soccer field on a relatively flat area and crew and passengers enjoyed playing in the evenings. We sometimes made our own entertainment and on 5 November celebrated the Melbourne Cup, the evening meal being billed as 'chicken and champagne in the paddock'. This was followed by the 'Nella Dan Stuck-In-The-Ice Steeplechase' at 8.00 pm. The five races on the card were run on a large board with six chess knights for horses. The horses' names were all topical, such as: '*Home for Christmas* — a candidate with slowly diminishing possibilities'; '*Sea Ice* — from *Horizon* to *Horizon*, out of *Bounds*, a persistent performer on a winter track'; '*TV* — out of *Good Videos*, from *Ant. Div.*, a guaranteed shocking performer'; and '*Chocolate Ration* — has not lived up to early promise'.

On 7 November the crew began using the anchor chains as saws to cut a gap between the hull and the ice. The anchors were dropped through holes in the ice forward of the bridge and winched up and down, the chains gradually cutting their way towards the bow. Our hopes of getting out were raised on 10 November when our meteorological forecaster, Jeff Wilson, predicted poor weather. A strong wind, combined with an ocean swell it could create, might break up the ice. I had never seen people so enthusiastic for bad weather! In 1967 *Nella* had been beset in the Casey region for thirty days and Arne Sørensen was on board at the time as an apprentice. It was now our fifteenth day stuck and, while enjoying our unusual experience, we had no desire to come near this record.

The weather was disappointingly good, particularly for Andy McGifford whose wife was expecting a baby soon after we were due back. Fired with the enthusiasm of a prospective

Left: Forecaster Jeff Wilson and Captain Arne Sørensen discuss the weather
Right: Using the chains as saws

While speaking over the radio, Knowles was asked if the propeller was back in the water. The ship supposedly had its stern in the air! We were at a loss to understand how such a false story had begun in Australia. During our forced stay we heard via personal cables a series of fanciful and entertaining reports about our situation, including that we had a food shortage. Besides the food for the voyage, the ship carried emergency rations in case it was trapped for a winter. Apart from some concern about the reaction of our relatives and friends to these stories, we were amused to learn what dire straits we were in.

In no danger, we continued the science programs and trying to free *Nella Dan*. *Nella* was now breaking her own way, but progress was slow because the smashed ice still filled the hole and took away momentum as she rammed the floe.

Another problem was that the ship ran up onto the solid ice and was unable to reverse off. To get her free required clearing snow and slush from around the bow. Helping *Nella*'s bosun, Benny Nielsen, and our deputy leader, Rick Burbury, clear floating lumps of ice, I walked about on the pieces which sank, but only till the water wet the soles of my boots. The other two being bigger had to stand on a firmer footing.

'How does he do that?' Rick demanded in light but frustrated tones.

'Oh, he's a believer!' Benny joked in reply. Walking over the ocean was easy; trying to sail across it was the problem!

The floe in which *Nella Dan* was captive varied in width from thirteen to twenty-two kilometres, but we were only 1.6 kilometres from the edge and could see a lead ahead. Though the water

father, he, along with Graham Blight and Greg Young, set to work digging the ice away from the stern of the ship. This small beginning quickly led to other people joining in and the eventual freeing of the ship from the vice-like grip of the ice. There was little effect when *Nella* was shunted backwards and forwards in the one-and-a-half-metre space, but the fact that the ship could move again encouraged us. The next day, the crew at the bow and the passengers at the stern worked enthusiastically using crowbars, spades, shovels, axes and any other available implement to

break and shift the 'Antarctic concrete'. Even the glaciologists' ice corers were pressed into service to make dotted lines of holes across the one-and-a-half to two-metre-thick ice. By the end of the day our efforts had gained a total of three metres.

Our besetment caused Antarctic Division to make the first of many revisions to the shipping schedule in an exceptional season. As expedition leader, Knowles Kerry was in regular contact with head office and on 12 November he was told that *Icebird* had been sent to pick up the Heard Island parties.

looked tantalisingly close, the distance was significant compared with the hole we had carved by 21 November — two ship-lengths long and three ship-widths wide. I received a telex from a friend with an appropriate quote from Psalm 139, verses 9 and 10:

If I rise on the wings of the
    dawn,
if I settle on the
    far side of the sea,
even there your hand will
    guide me,
your right hand will hold me
    fast.

The Captain's Dinner was held on 23 November and this occasion was also used to celebrate *Nella Dan*'s twenty-fifth year of Antarctic service. She had spent her first season of 1961/62 and every austral summer since in service to ANARE. At a restaurant in Hobart, dignitaries from J. Lauritzen (the ship's owner), Antarctic Division, the Department of Science and other guests were celebrating *Nella Dan*'s silver jubilee, but without the guest of honour who should have been berthed at a nearby wharf.

On 25 November I was disappointed to hear that head office had told us to stop breaking out. We were making up to ten metres an hour in metre-thick ice, but using far more fuel than when stationary. If we kept going, the return to Hobart would have to be a slow one at our most economical speed, eight knots. We were to wait for *Icebird* which that day left Heard Island and was heading towards us. It was estimated *Icebird* would reach us at about the same time that we would have been able to extricate ourselves. A blizzard to break up the ice remained our only hope of getting free before *Icebird* arrived, but a decent blow failed to materialise and we continued drifting up and down the coast with the ice.

Left: Crew and passengers successfully digging out *Nella Dan*
Above: Using an empty drum and a winch to scoop up ice and snow

Icebird's advance towards us was slowed, firstly by having to shelter behind an iceberg from force 10 winds and then on 1 December their voyage leader, Graeme Manning, advised us they were 'beset' in shifting pack ice. Recognising a sudden change in conditions they had tried to get out immediately, but *Icebird* became stuck within ten minutes. A river of ice slid past them and pressure was put on the hull which creaked under the strain. Graeme and *Icebird*'s captain, Ewald Brune, made contingency plans to evacuate everyone to nearby Cape Ann

and *Nella Dan* if *Icebird* had to be abandoned, but fortunately the pressure relented and *Icebird* made her way to safety.

At this time we received news that showed we were not the only one with shipping strife. The British Antarctic Survey ship, *John Biscoe*, had also become beset in Antarctic waters and had been abandoned. After the danger had passed, people returned to the ship and it continued sailing.

A party from *Icebird* flew across to *Nella Dan* on 2 December to discuss our situation. Head office had directed as many people as possible to be transferred to *Icebird* in case she was unable to free *Nella Dan*. Twenty passengers were flown across on the third, leaving a minimum scientific crew behind. People were reluctant to leave their comrades and *Nella*: they felt dedicated to the ship and their work programs.

That morning I read a press release from Antarctic Division which stated: 'Twenty scientists from the stranded Antarctic ship *Nella Dan* were today lifted from the vessel by helicopter and transferred to *Icebird*'. No-one had left at that stage and it was not until the afternoon that we fulfilled the news. Conditions on *Icebird* were overcrowded with the new arrivals and some people had to sleep on the bench seats in the mess. The sixteen of us who were pleased to be staying on *Nella Dan* were flown to *Icebird* and given a three-minute telephone call to home

on the ship's satellite telephone link, courtesy of Antarctic Division.

Between *Icebird* and *Nella Dan* lay a relatively easy path through some pack ice and then along a lead of clear water. The weather was sunny with little wind, and Captain Brune estimated that it would take two hours to reach opposite *Nella Dan* and twenty-four hours to break through to her. Those on both ships were keen

for *Icebird* to make an attempt, but the decision was made in Australia for us — there was the possibility *Icebird* could be delayed further by bad weather after breaking us out or might get caught again and the risk was not to be taken. *Icebird* then left on her way to Hobart via the originally scheduled stops at the ice edges off Mawson and Davis.

On *Nella Dan* we now waited for the arrival of the Japanese ship, *Shirase*. In late November Japan had generously offered to assist us by sending *Shirase* which would be sailing via Fremantle in Western Australia to their Antarctic base Syowa, west of *Nella Dan*. *Shirase* was a true icebreaker — unlike *Nella Dan* and *Icebird* which were only ice-strengthened ships — and was quite new, having been commissioned in 1982. When *Shirase* sailed from Fremantle

Above: *Shirase* approaches *Nella Dan*
Left: *Icebird*
Above right: *Shirase* frees *Nella Dan*
Right: Captain Sørensen, First Officer Magnus Olafsson and Voyage Leader Knowles Kerry on *Nella*'s bridge

she carried extra fuel, fresh fruit, vegetables and some unofficial items for us. Our medical officer, Hugh Jones, had sent an urgent message to his wife at Fremantle who hastily bought magazines, newspapers and paperbacks and rushed these — along with some homemade cooking — to the ship before it sailed.

I was filled with anticipation and a sense of excitement when *Shirase* appeared as a ghostly shape on the horizon on the evening of 13 December. Snow had fallen on and off during the day and the bridge became lined with people watching *Shirase* work her way towards us through the gloom. She stopped for the night six kilometres away and resumed her approach the next morning.

The icebreaker had experienced little trouble advancing through the pack ice until it reached our floe. For the first time ever it was forced to back up and run at ice instead of being able to plough straight through it. Although the floe was only two to three metres thick on average, there

were the pressure ridges to contend with where the ice had been heaped up and these extended deep below the surface. A diver had measured ice twenty metres thick at one place next to *Nella Dan*. The closer *Shirase* came the more she was slowed, particularly by one formidable barrier which took an hour to pound through.

It was not until 7.00 pm that *Shirase* had passed the tough section and was heading

to go across our bow. The might of the ship had begun to rupture the surrounding ice and a long split extended out from its track, ran in front of *Nella* and off to our right for hundreds of metres. A small group of Adelie penguins two hundred metres in front of *Shirase* were about to become involved in the saga of our release. I made the following diary entry of the event:

The last two shunts *Shirase* made were really impressive — a sheer display of power and quite unforgettable. During the second last push, plates of sea ice fifteen metres long and ten wide were thrust up at angles from her sides and the penguins ran for their lives until the approaching ship slowed and stopped. *Shirase* backed up for what was to be her last run. When she hit the broken floe, the ice parted and the ship powered through with staggering immensity. The piece of ice the Adelies were on was speared forward and the penguins fled in terror from the juggernaut, diving off the far end.

The icebreaker continued on past our bow and at this historic moment of release after forty-eight days beset we looked across at *Shirase*'s enormous helideck to see people playing tennis! The ice in front of us opened and we were able to follow in *Shirase*'s wake. We had all enjoyed our unplanned stay, but it was good to be on the move and heading for home. We felt pleased but, strangely, not elated.

Following *Shirase* along a lead was simple, but we were brought to a stop soon after entering the pack where we could not force our way

of around 150 tonnes was dragged over and made fast to two bollards on the foredeck.

The strain was taken. *Nella* moved forward a little, but stopped again. The rope grew visibly thinner. There were loud, rhythmic banging sounds a few seconds apart as if someone were hitting the deck with a sledge-hammer. With a deafening bang and a bright shower of sparks, the rear bollard was slammed forward and the front one ripped from the deck, flung against the inside of the bow, ricocheted high into the air and back twenty metres where it

skywards in a flurry of paint chips. No-one had been allowed near the front while the tow was in progress, but when the bollard flew so far back it had some of the crew leaping for cover.

The Japanese asked if we wanted to try again, but Captain Sørensen declined unless the ice was pushed out of the way first. 'We're running short of bollards,' he quipped. *Shirase* broke up more of the ice around *Nella Dan* before we stopped for the night at 3.00 am after a rather dramatic day.

Operations began again

through the broken ice which choked her neatly carved channel. The 30,000 horsepower *Shirase* ran over the top of solid ice, crushing it under her hull and spewing it out behind. The 2,520 horsepower *Nella Dan* could not run over the ice and needed somewhere to push it. *Shirase* circled and broke up the ice about us, but *Nella* was still unable to make any headway. *Shirase*'s captain, Atsushi Kurata, then suggested they tow us. It was 12.05 am and overcast but still light when they fired a rocket line across to us and a huge towrope with a breaking strain

smashed a wooden pallet before hitting the deck. The two-hundred-metre-long rope recoiled like a stretched rubber band and shot back towards *Shirase*, not touching the water till it was halfway across.

It was all over before the impact of it registered on my mind. I was riveted for a second, stunned by this spectacular incident before excitedly taking in the detail of what had happened. When the bollard hit the inside of the prow it chopped and fractured the ten millimetre steel plate sending one of the two spotlights mounted there popping

later in the morning when *Shirase* used her backwash to clear the ice between the two ships. *Nella Dan* was only able to follow for a short distance because of pieces of ice up to fifteen metres across that bobbed up behind *Shirase* and barred our way. Another tow was attempted, this time utilising four bollards instead of two. All cameras were at the ready as the strain was taken, but the bollards held and we were on our way. *Nella Dan* then proceeded under her own power most of the time and the towrope only became taut occasionally.

Nearly three hours later both ships were still moving well when *Shirase* turned slightly, pulling *Nella*'s bow sideways. This set *Nella Dan* swaying on the towrope and, as I watched, another bollard hurtled into the air and the rope parted. The bollard dented the deck when it landed and we were left with a short length of rope which appeared to have been partly cut by the ragged steel before snapping.

By this time the ice conditions were light enough that a tow was unnecessary and at 5.15 pm *Nella* docked alongside *Shirase* after reaching a large polynya. Amid much cheering and exchanging of greetings, a gangplank was put across. We received our groceries, the items from Hugh's wife, and the fuel was pumped into *Nella Dan*'s tanks.

Tours were arranged of both ships and *Nella Dan* swarmed with Oriental visitors. I found *Shirase* a complete contrast to *Nella Dan* and not only in size and power. She was a military-crewed ship and was fitted with every conceivable piece of modern equipment. The most surprising thing for me was the barber shop — complete with rotating red, white and blue pole outside the door! Two large helicopters and a smaller one were housed in hangars in front of their vast helideck. One of their pilots looked down on our rear deck and asked, 'That is your helideck?'

'Yes,' was the reply.

'Aaah, you must be very brave!' he said. For one of our helicopters to land in its parking position a blade from the other had to be removed to allow enough space.

Left: The tow rope from *Shirase*, *Nella Dan* under tow and the torn-out bollards
Above: Howard Burton examines the damage after another try
Right: *Shirase* and *Nella Dan*

Left and above: *Shirase* and *Nella Dan* docked together

As a farewell gift from *Nella Dan*, a presentation was made to the crew of *Shirase* of one of the torn-out bollards. Morten Qvist, a motorman from *Nella*, had welded 'Nella Dan 15/12/85' across its top. The Japanese were delighted with this trophy, and took turns at being photographed while sitting astride it.

At 8.40 pm people on both ships lined the rails, waving and calling as if farewelling old friends as *Nella* cast off from *Shirase*'s side. We came in behind *Shirase* and followed her out through the thinning pack ice. At 9.15 the next morning, with blasts from *Nella Dan*'s horn, we parted from our hospitable Japanese friends and headed in opposite directions.

We were once again in the 'wobbly stuff' after the calm of the pack ice, but the crew were pleased to be in the open sea. A few days before Christmas, a telex arrived from the ex-*Nella* people on *Icebird* who were almost home. They had composed a Christmas carol for us and instructed that it was to be sung to the tune of 'I Saw Three Ships Go Sailing By'. Four of the verses are listed here:

> We saw a ship go sailing by,
>   sailing by, sailing by,
> We saw a ship go sailing by
> On Christmas day in the
>   morning.
>
> The ship was red with flanks
>   rubbed raw, flanks rubbed
>   raw, flanks rubbed raw,
> The ship was red with flanks
>   rubbed raw,
> Her mooring lines all broken.
>
> And on the deck were gaping
>   holes, gaping holes, gaping
>   holes,
> And on the deck were gaping
>   holes
> Where bollards had been
>   standing.
>
> The crew and boffins made
>   whoopee, made whoopee,
>   made whoopee,
> The crew and boffins made
>   whoopee,
> With Christmas fare and
>   champers.

They returned to Hobart on 23 December where Andy McGifford was introduced to his new son. We were still somewhere in the Southern Ocean and had an enjoyable Christmas on board *Nella Dan*. Santa called during the night bringing me chocolate, liquorice allsorts, a paperback and two pairs of ANARE-issue socks! My best gift, though, came on Christmas Day when I was able to talk with home on the ham radio.

We sighted Tasmania on Saturday 28 December and dropped anchor after midnight in the moonlit Derwent River. Breakfast was at 7.00 am and around 8.00 am the pilot, customs officers, the then Minister for Science, the Hon. Barry Jones, and the Director of Antarctic Division, Jim Bleasel, came on board. *Nella Dan* sailed to the wharf where we returned the greeting of families, friends and the press by throwing snowballs at them, brought from Antarctica specially for the occasion.

With newspaper, radio and television reporters on the dock, it seemed we were big news throughout Australia, but most of us were not directly involved in this moment of fame. As I stepped ashore, I felt it was the end of an unforgettable and exciting adventure that had been shared with good friends.

9
Bunger Hills

LUGGING MY GEAR UP the gangplank, I boarded *Nella Dan* again, six days after arriving back from the besetment voyage. Howard Burton had also been on the last trip and we returned to familiar Cabin 8. I even had the same bunk and felt as if I had never left.

Howard was on his way to Davis for the rest of the summer and I was in a group of twenty-two going to the Bunger Hills to set up a new summer base called Edgeworth David and do scientific work. My job was photographer instead of electronics engineer and I was to print black-and-white aerial photographs of the Bunger Hills area and document the activities of the expedition. *Nella Dan*'s late return had postponed the sailing date for Bunger Hills by twenty-four days. There was to have been three weeks between my two trips providing time to practise with new equipment, but now I could only read instruction manuals on the way south.

We reached ice-covered Mill Island at the edge of the

Shackleton Ice Shelf on the evening of 12 January 1986 and were stopped there by sea ice which had not broken out. The ship had sailed from the sombreness of dark cloud into a sun-bathed world where flocks of snow petrels flew about dazzling icebergs. In the dark blue water by the edge of the continuous white sheet of fast ice, whales broke the surface to breathe, the puffs of spray from their blows drifting

lazily away after they dived.

The ice shelf at the eastern end of Mill Island was two or three metres high and would have made unloading convenient. The sea ice prevented us from reaching this natural wharf, so we sailed the length of Mill Island looking for another suitable place and found a bay (later named Nella Dan Bay) formed by the western end of the island and the protruding Scott Glacier. The ship was moored the following morning to sea ice joining the side of the glacier.

Rod Ledingham, the Bunger Hills field party leader, and I selected a site for a coastal depot before flying over the Shackleton Ice Shelf to Bunger Hills. The other two helicopters accompanied us, one carrying two drums of fuel and the second, Arne Sørensen and Tom Maggs, the voyage leader. On arriving, we checked at the old Polish station of Dobrowolski which had last been manned in the 1978-79 season. It was rumoured there might be a group there for the summer, but we found it deserted. Rod

Above: Assembling a hut
for Bunger Hills on the sea ice

and I then examined several areas, looking for a suitable site for Edgeworth David. We chose a spot by a shallow, freshwater lake near the frozen sea. Although the ship lay sixty-seven kilometres from us at the coast, the Shackleton Ice Shelf which separated us was floating on the ocean. Between the inland edge of the shelf and the rocky hills is what could best be described as an inland sea, parts of which melt if the summer is warm. We sighted some Weddell seals and wondered whether they were an isolated population or had swum in under the shelf, coming up to breathe in the crevasses along the way.

We returned to *Nella Dan* where everyone was busy unloading cargo onto the sea ice. The helicopters then flew it to the nearby coastal depot on the ice shelf. Red fibreglass huts, which we called apple huts because of their shape and colour, were to make up the base and they were assembled beside the ship and carried to the depot slung under the helicopters. I took particular care helping build one of these huts that had been made black and was to serve as my darkroom.

An advance party consisting of Jeannie Ledingham, Brian Murphy, Tiernan McNamara and I were flown to the Edgeworth David site on 14 January. The next day the weather was too windy for flying and the evening meal on the ship was

interrupted when the ice *Nella* was tied to began to break up. All hands hurried outside and reloaded gear onto the ship.

The first loads from the coastal depot arrived at our tents on the 17th and opening one box revealed a microwave oven. It was thoughtful of someone to send it, but they had forgotten the extension cord to run to the ship. Rod and Graeme Currie arrived at Edgeworth David and the six of us levelled sites on a rocky slope ready for the huts. *Nella Dan* sailed that evening, leaving us to our own devices.

The following day, work began in earnest setting up base camp and at lunchtime two helicopters appeared as tiny black dots carrying the first of the huts. As their silhouettes grew larger, I noticed that one hut seemed further below its aircraft than a moment before and I suddenly realised it was falling. Alarm came over me in the drawn-out seconds it took to plunge four hundred metres before disappearing behind the horizon of the nearby ice shelf and smashing to pieces.

'Which one was it?' I called quickly to Rod who held a radio. He spoke briefly with the pilots.

'The black one,' he answered. I was speechless. I did not know whether to rage or weep. Of our six huts this was the only one that was indispensable, now lost because of a faulty latch on the helicopter sling hook. The Antarctic factor had struck again!

I quickly saw the funny side of this personal disaster and set about modifying one of the red huts. Using black plastic from packing crates, I covered one panel section on the outside of the hut and then hung curtains of plastic inside to give a small, wedge-shaped and light-tight room. Inside this I loaded and developed film while printing the photographs was done in the main body of the hut. The red light which filtered through the walls was 'safe' for the printing paper and did not expose it. After installing an enlarger and an automatic print processor alongside the blacked-out room, there was enough space to squeeze in a small table and my bed.

Two of the other apple huts were extended by splitting them in half and adding straight panels in the centre, thus creating 'melons'. One melon was used as a kitchen/mess and the other for sleeping. In one of the remaining apples were three bunks and the last hut housed the radio and meteorological equipment. The sleeping huts could not contain everyone so Rod, Jeannie, Graeme and our meteorologist, John Nairn, braved the weather in tents. A shower room was constructed by 'Dodgy Brothers' from packing cases and the remains of the black apple. Inside hung a canvas camp shower which we filled with hot water from a drum that sat over a fire of aircraft fuel.

Soon after we settled in, a skua claimed the camp as his own and trained the inhabitants to handfeed him. Salami was his favourite food, though fingers were almost taken too if the skua-feeder was not careful.

Above, left and right: Helicopters — the key means of transport
Top right: A meal in warm weather

We named him Edgeworth and his mate, who joined him later, was called David. This pair begged at the door of the mess and ran along behind people like dogs, hoping for a meal.

Twelve people were permanently based at Edgeworth David with the remainder of our complement in five groups that spent varying amounts of time in the field studying the structural geology, geomorphology and biology of the area. The helicopters were used to shift their camps as they moved about the hills. Survey work was done by a National Mapping team who also took the colour and black-and-white aerial photographs. I developed the black-and-white film and made prints to cover areas that the field parties were interested in. Using the photographs, the structural geologists, for instance, could identify features and go straight to them instead of having to comb the hills.

I left my dark hole for a while and joined some of the geologists in the field, spending six days with them in the

Above: Brian Murphy feeding David the skua
Left: Peter Stahle taking a moss sample
Top right: The photographic darkroom
Right: Jeannie Ledingham, the medical officer, helping set up the kitchen

Above: Edgeworth David, evening
Left: Author Rowan Butler in the darkroom
Bottom: The official opening!
Right: The geologist's field camp

south-east of the hills. The countryside we walked through was near the Antarctic plateau and was steeper and more rugged than the coastal areas. The hills were rounded and there were patches of smooth bedrock which shone in the sun. These worn surfaces had been polished by rocks grinding over them, pushed along for perhaps hundreds of kilometres under the moving icecap. The ice later retreated off the hills, leaving them scattered with debris varying in size from huge boulders to powder called rock flour. The only vegetation to be found was lichen and rare patches of moss.

After a day walking with Kurt Stüwe, one of the geologists, I wrote:

No placid lake scenes as I write tonight. The wind is shaking the wildly flapping tent and the snow striking the fly sounds like someone is flinging fine gravel at it. Overall there is a continuous, distant roar from the wind racing through the bare hills.

Our tents are in a sheltered spot, so we are protected from the main blow and there are lulls when the tents sit quietly, but the roar is incessant.

The day had begun in marked contrast to this when I left camp that morning to go after Kurt. Along the way, the small lakes which were cradled in the barren, boulder-strewn hills lay perfectly still in a stony silence.

It was as if someone had switched off the world. When I stopped to listen to the noise-lessness, I had to take off my pack because it creaked too loudly when I breathed.

My clumping footfalls desecrated this exciting, inaudible world as I stepped from rock to rock, eventually catching up with Kurt. A faint breeze sprang up. By the afternoon a wind was blowing and as we walked into it towards the plateau it strengthened, making us lean forward as we struggled against it. Climbing over the last rise to where the rock gave way to endless ice, we were exposed to the full ferocity of the wind. I winced as snow granules pelted my face and it

Left: A frozen waterfall
Above: Chinese geologist, Ding Puquan, on a boulder worn when pushed by the icecap
Right: Kurt Stüwe

Above: Ice on rocks from spray
Below: Bad weather at camp

was impossible to stand
upright. I kept getting blown
backwards even when crouched
or crawling. My pack helped
weigh me down but also caught
the wind, throwing me off
balance. This was no place to
be for too long, no matter how
thrilling it was, and we made a
strategic withdrawal to the
comparative shelter of the hills.

Our return to camp was
hastened by a strong tail wind.

Talking to Graeme Currie
over the radio before I returned
to Edgeworth David, I was told
the latest rumour — that
Icebird had trouble with her
main drive gear and was returning to Hobart after having left
there only five days previously.
The story seemed too ludicrous
and I did not believe it.
However, later that night it was
confirmed as being true and the

AAP telex news bulletin we
received for 18 February read:

Hobart: The Antarctic supply
ship, *Icebird*, is limping back
to Hobart tonight after suffering a major mechanical failure
during her final voyage south
for the summer season.

The mechanical break-
down has dealt a further blow
to the Antarctic Division's
summer resupply schedule,
which underwent hasty revi-
sion late last year after the

Above: The view from the author's tent
Below: Glaciated pavement

supply ship, *Nella Dan*, was locked in ice for seven weeks.

The *Icebird* was about 1,200 nautical miles south of Hobart, bound for Antarctica, when her main drive gear linking the engine and propeller shaft broke last night . . .

Another alteration to the shipping schedule was required and *Nella Dan* was diverted from her last port of call of Albany in Western Australia to Hobart. She was supposed to be returning home to Denmark, but was chartered for an extra voyage. *Nella* sailed from Hobart on 24 February and the following day rendezvoused with *Icebird* which was still returning at reduced speed to avoid further damage. Mail was transferred to *Nella Dan* and *Icebird* reached port on 26 February. New gears were sent from Germany and, after the repairs were completed, *Icebird* sailed on the last voyage of the season on 13 March.

The shipping for the season had been somewhat of a nightmare with seven amendments to the original schedule. The changes had to take account of such major contingencies as *Nella Dan*'s besetment, the quick chartering of HMAS *Stalwart* to do *Nella Dan*'s Macquarie Island relief voyage, and

Icebird's forced return. Other organisations continued to have difficulties, too: the Greenpeace ship, *Greenpeace*, failed to reach Antarctica because of heavy ice conditions and the 'In The Footsteps of Scott, Antarctic Expedition 1984-86' lost their ship, *Southern Quest*, when it was caught between two icefloes and crushed. All the upset programs reminded me of Proverbs 16.9: 'You may make your plans, but God directs your actions.'

Despite the Antarctic Division's press releases describing *Nella Dan*'s relief voyage as 'a race against time' and 'a race against the sea ice' before it prevented her reaching us and the two bases of Davis and Mawson, we were not particularly worried and, if anything, found the situation entertaining.

I had my own voyage problems when I was shipwrecked with the 'Bunger Navy'. Its flagship was an inflatable boat used by one of the biologists, David Hay. I went out in it on a lake to photograph him using a mechanical grab which took samples from the bottom. All went well until we approached some fast ice at one end of the lake. Here the

Above and left: Reading the telex news

outboard motor failed completely and a strengthening wind blew us into small floes and pieces of ice which had banked against the fast ice.

The inflatable was in danger of being holed by jagged ice and the wind was strong enough to thwart our efforts to row against it. The slurry of broken ice stopped us from successfully pushing our way with the oars towards the shore, so I suggested the only alternative was get out and walk back over the jigsaw of floes. These were slippery and constantly awash from small waves, but we carefully stepped from one to the next, pulling and pushing the boat along in the water. At a gap too large to jump across safely, we ferried ourselves one at a time on a smaller piece of rocking ice. Over the last twenty metres to shore the ice was too fragmented to walk on, but it was more sheltered and we managed to row to safety. Our floe-hopping exercise had been risky but fun. I was happy I had not ended up in the lake — even though it was supposed to be a relatively warm three to five degrees centigrade!

Above: David Hay
Right: Taking an algae sample

The surveyors' work took them further afield than the Bunger Hills. They visited the Obruchev Hills and other ice-free areas, including Possession Rocks where Brian Murphy found an old cane and a semi-circle of rocks against a ledge. Inside this border was a piece of sash cord. We presumed these relics to be from a depot laid by a group from Mawson's 1911-13 Australasian Antarctic Expedition.

The AAE's Western Base Party had wintered on the western end of the Shackleton Ice Shelf while the main expedition group was at Common-wealth Bay, 2,050 kilometres to the east. Frank Wild, who was in charge of the Western Base Party, three other men and three dogs made a return manhaul trip eastwards between 30 October 1912 and 6 January 1913. They mapped the coast-line and sighted ice-free land in the distance, but were turned back by the heavily crevassed Denman Glacier, poor sledging conditions and limited rations. They had made a depot at Pos-session Rocks and returned to it on Christmas Day 1912. The land which they had seen was later named Bunger Hills after Lieutenant Commander D.E.

Above: An aerial view of pack ice. A house would fit on most of these floes
Right: Removing a blade so the third helicopter can land

Bunger, USN, who landed there in a seaplane on an unfrozen lake in February 1947.

Our activities for this first summer of a planned three-year program for Australia in the Bunger Hills came to a close on 5 March 1986 when three helicopters flew us out to the waiting *Nella Dan*. For the third time that season I was sailing on 'the little red ship' and that night as I dined in the mess I watched the towering

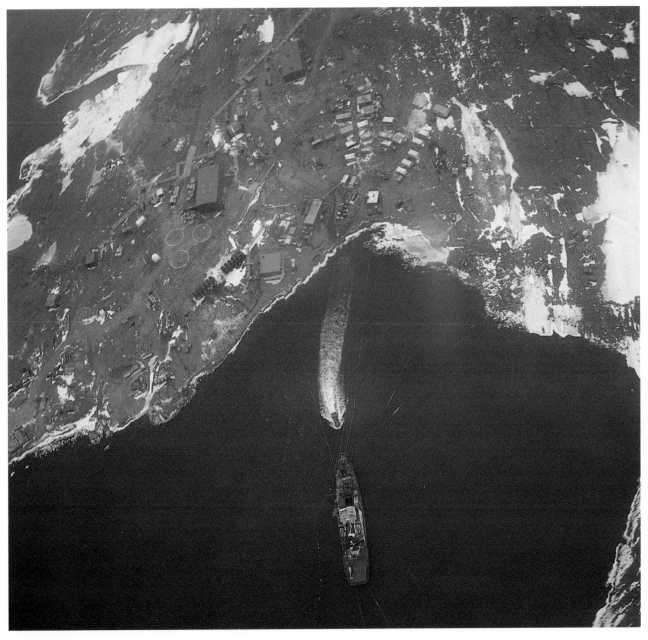

Left: Willy Pedersen dropping *Nella Dan*'s anchor
Above: An aerial view of Mawson with *Nella Dan* in Horseshoe Harbour

white cliffs along the side of Mill Island glide by. No restaurant could have provided such a unique and impressive view.

We sailed to Davis and picked up expeditioners from there who were returning home. On 10 March we left, not retracing our inward path through heavy pack, but heading north-east, the satellite photograph showing clearer water there. That night *Nella Dan* stopped amongst pack ice

and a tangle of icebergs when it started snowing, making visibility poor. We continued on the following day, travelling a circuitous route in search of open sea. Some people on board, as well as those at head office, began to fear we might become beset again, and it was now the end of the season when there was little chance of the sea ice breaking up before the following summer. There were areas of new ice forming and we could see that the floes were freezing together. The voyage leader, Ian Marchant, had been stuck for a week on *Nanok S* in 1983 after leaving Davis and at

the same time of year. It was not until the morning of the 12th that the pack began to thin and in the early afternoon everyone's concern was relieved when we reached open water.

Nella Dan slid into Horseshoe Harbour at Mawson late on Thursday 13 March and on Friday morning we were allowed ashore. I spent the time around the station looking at the new buildings and other changes. The Red Shed was now occupied and the rooms were spacious and modern compared with the old dongas. I was surprised by the number

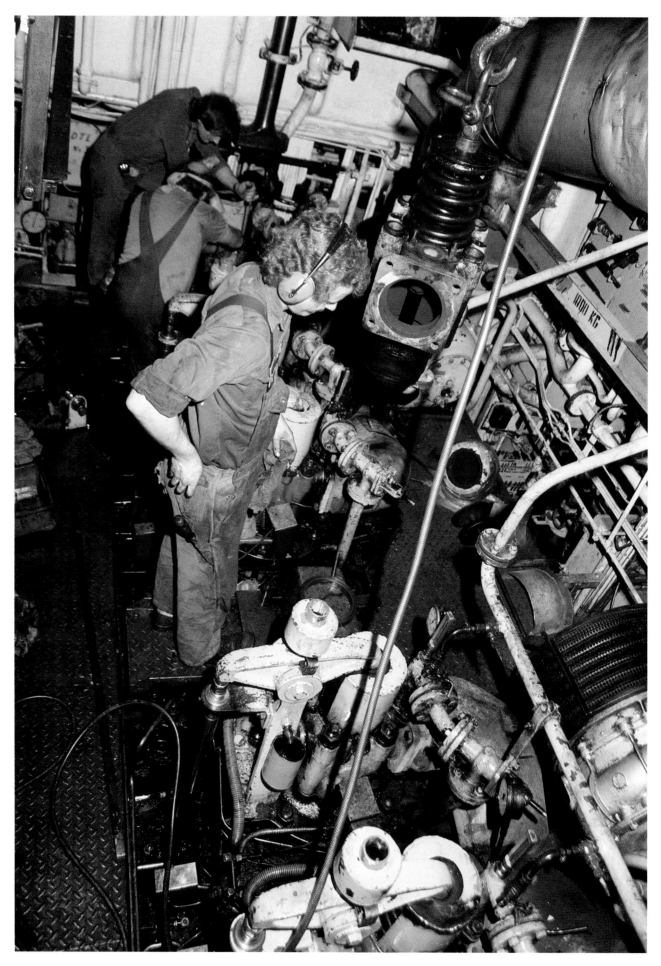

of trivial things I recognised
and was touched with a sense
of nostalgia when I looked up
and down the coast from Aeronomy, a view I had always
enjoyed. My tour could not be
complete without visiting the
dogs and I patted/wrestled each
in turn, paying particular attention to those I had worked
with in 1981.

We made ready to leave
Antarctica on Saturday and the
ship's Chief Engineer, Erling
Helslev, gave me the privilege
of starting Olga, *Nella Dan*'s
engine. At 6.55 pm we sailed
from Mawson with more
returning expeditioners. *Nella
Dan* was overcrowded, with
two sittings for meals being
required, and people were allo-
cated beds on couches or
floors.

Sailing up Kista Strait
towards Welch Island and then
out to sea, I saw the expanse of
coastline around Mawson and
its immediate hinterland spreading before me. The low sun
highlighted the form and
texture of the plateau —
crevassed mounds, glassy slopes
and flow lines where the ice
streamed downhill to the sea.

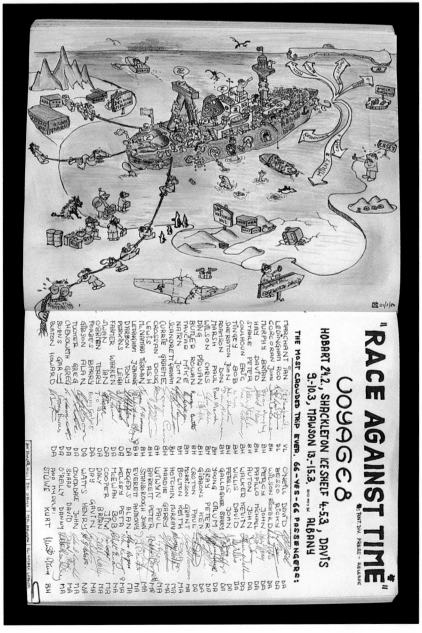

Left: *Nella Dan*'s engine, Olga
Above: Icing-up in cold weather
Right: Passengers' log book

149

Standing out from a background of black cloud were the mountains, skirted by orange-pink drift blowing in the wind. The David and Casey Ranges smoked with swirling drift which curled away to the west, having cleared the ridgetops. In the foreground, two Antarctic fulmars glided behind the ship and a group of Adelie penguins bobbed up and down on a miniature iceberg. Antarctica was 'declaring the glory of God... proclaiming the work of his hands'.

Each visit has reinforced my impression of Antarctica's beauty. I am continually captivated by the diversity and richness of its colour, landscape, wildlife and weather. Even the mishaps and uncertainties add an ingredient of excitement. And there is always the anticipation that the next season in this vast, little-known continent will reveal new wonders.

Above: Welch Island, Antarctica, with Mount Henderson (left) and Onley Hill (right) behind

Appendix A:

Nella Dan

NELLA DAN SANK off Macquarie Island in her own time and way. The report in *The Age*, Melbourne, of 26 December 1987 quoted Dylan Thomas:

Do not go gentle into that good night,
Old age should burn and rave at close of day;
Rage, rage against the dying of the light.

Old age she had. The 1987/88 summer was her twenty-seventh consecutive season working for ANARE after being launched in 1961. When *Nella Dan* went, it was the passing of a class of ship — and an era.

In her later years of service, she worked longer seasons than in her early days, due to Australia's increased activities in Antarctica. I had the privilege of travelling on parts of all three voyages of her longest season, beginning when she first sailed for Antarctic waters from Hobart on 15 September 1985 and ending when she made her last return to Albany on 26 March 1986. In the early parts of these extended seasons, she occasionally had difficulties with the heavy ice conditions which prevail at such times and some people incorrectly thought her unsafe. A particularly sturdy vessel, many who knew her would have preferred to be on *Nella Dan* rather than on some of the more modern ships if stuck in ice.

Nella Dan travelled some 515,400 nautical miles (954,500 km) during eighty-seven voyages south (eighty-five in service to ANARE) and five trial marine science voyages. By the end of 1982, she had travelled a total of 1,110,000 nautical miles (2,055,720 km).

Nella's Danish crew were always friendly and a few had virtually made their home on board — for example Benny Nielsen, the bosun, who sailed the last fourteen years on her to Antarctica. In nine of those years, he also sailed on *Nella* to Greenland, during the Northern Hemisphere's

summer. Only two chief stewards served on the Antarctic voyages: Sven Nielsen for the first thirteen years and Ruben Nielsen for the remaining fourteen.

The beginning of the end came for *Nella Dan* when she went aground at Buckles Bay, Macquarie Island on 3 December 1987. She was refloated and her owner, J. Lauritzen, planned to repair her, but a judgment was made that it would be unsafe to tow her back, so it was decided to scuttle her.

The ship's bell and the triangle which was used to summon passengers for meals were two of the few items saved from the collection of memorabilia which had been packed and was ready to be taken off. Most of this was left behind when *Nella* was hastily abandoned because of the fear she was going to capsize. This failed to eventuate and shortly before she was to be boarded again the following morning, Christmas Eve, a fire broke out, preventing plans to take her treasures and then scuttle her.

Nella Dan underwent a Viking funeral before slipping below the Southern Ocean to the true graveyard of ships. On hearing this news, many of those who had travelled in her and loved her, shed more than one tear for a vessel that was more than a legendary ship — she was a grand lady.

Owner:	J. Lauritzen
Built:	1961 at Aalborg, Denmark
Weight:	2,193 tonnes gross
Length:	75.24 metres
Max. Speed:	12.5 knots

Nella Dan was named after Nell Law, the wife of Dr Phillip Law, Director of the Antarctic Division from 1949 to 1966.

She now lies at the bottom of the Southern Ocean at 54° 37.5' S, 159° 13.3' E.

Appendix B:
Mawson winterers 1981 and Casey winterers 1984

ANARE 1981 Mawson wintering expeditioners:

Gordon Ashcroft	Construction Foreman
Paul Butler	Officer in Charge
Rowan Butler	Electronics Engineer
Derry Craig	Diesel Mechanic
Rick Crowle	Communications Officer
Graham Dadswell	Communications Officer
Don Dettman	Diesel Mechanic
Heinz Dittloff	Radio Technical Officer
Wal Elliot	Diesel Mechanic
Rick Flemming	Carpenter
Geoff Fulton	Meteorological Observer
John Gough	Plumber
Mark Haste	Carpenter
George Hedanek	Plant Inspector
Peter Jacob	Physicist
Norm Jones	Physicist
Ron Kennedy	Carpenter
Peter Longden	Medical Officer
Peter McLennan	Meteorological Technical Officer
Rod MacLeod	Physicist
Ross McShane	Communications Officer
Alan Marks	Geophysicist
Mark Meyer	Senior Meteorological Observer
Andrew Murray	Physicist
Steve Musgrove	Electrician
John Peiniger	Electronics Engineer
Terry Rose	Communications Officer
George Thomson	Plumber
Henry Weiss	Electrician
Allan Winter	Cook
Stuart Wolfe	Radio Technical Officer
Bob Yeoman	Carpenter

ANARE 1984 Casey wintering expeditioners:

Bruce Adam	Medical Officer
Garry Barclay	Diesel Mechanic
Brian Baxter	Diesel Mechanic
Mic Bence	Communications Officer
Russell Brand	Diesel Mechanic
Gary Burton	Plant Inspector
Rowan Butler	Electronics Engineer
Jim Clarke	Surveyor
Neil Conrick	Carpenter
Qin Dahe	Glaciologist
Ray Etherington	Electrician
Dave Grant	Senior Meteorological Observer
Ken Hankinson	Communications Officer
Peter Hesketh	Construction Foreman
Allan Hiscock	Plumber
Trevor Lloyd	Radio Technical Officer
Jeff Longworth	Electrician
Sandy McCombie	Carpenter
Andy Martin	Plumber
Paul Matthews	Plumber
Dave Nicholas	Meteorological Observer
Peter Norris-Smith	Radio Technical Officer
Bill Robinson	Cook
Jim Semmens	Plant Operator
Merv Steel	Communications Officer
Eric Szworak	Meteorological Technical Officer
Rik Thwaites	Glaciologist
Brian Whiteley	Officer in Charge
Andy Wood	Diesel Mechanic
Bob Yeoman	Carpenter

Appendix C:
Traverse statistics

THESE DETAILS OF the 1984 autumn and spring glaciological traverses from Casey are taken with permission from the Casey glaciology 1984 Operations Report by Rik Thwaites of Antarctic Division.

Autumn traverse
8 March — 5 May 1984, 59 days.

Usage of field time, both trains:

Travelling:	35 days
Taking measurements:	9 days
Mechanical repairs:	9 days
Blizzard conditions:	6 days

Traverse length: 1,040 km

Average distance travelled per day:

March:	33 km	Moderate loads, mostly firm surface.
April:	19 km	Double-hauling heavy load, many breakages, soft, rough conditions.
May:	27 km	Double-hauling heavy load, firm surface.

Spring traverse
15 September 1984 — 5 January 1985, 113 days.

Usage of field time:

☐ *Flash* train
Travelling:	55 days
Taking measurements:	38 days
Automatic weather station work:	5 days
Blizzard conditions:	15 days

Traverse length: 2,120 km

☐ *Gordon* train
Travelling:	59 days
Taking measurements:	13 days
Automatic weather station work:	24 days
Blizzard conditions:	17 days

Traverse length: 2,260 km

Average distance travelled per day:

September:	31 km	Moderate loads travelling out.
October:	26 km	Moderate loads, measurements taken.
November:	33 km	Measurements taken, return.
December & January:	49 km	Lighter loads, measurements taken.

Bibliography

ARMSTRONG, T., ROBERTS, B. & SWITHINBANK, C. *Illustrated Glossary of Snow and Ice*. The Scott Polar Research Institute, Cambridge, 1966

BÉCHERVAISE, J. *Antarctica: The Last Horizon*. Cassell, Melbourne, 1979

BICKEL, L. *This Accursed Land*. MacMillan, Melbourne, 1977

BUTLER, R. *Personal Diaries*. 1980-81, 1984-86

CHESTER, J. *Going To Extremes: Project Blizzard and Australia's Antarctic Heritage*. Doubleday, Sydney, 1986

CHIPMAN, E. *Australians In The Frozen South: Living & Working in Antarctica*. Thomas Nelson, Melbourne, 1978

CUMPSTON, J. *Macquarie Island*. Publication No.93, ANARE Scientific Reports, Series A (1) Narrative. Antarctic Division, Department of External Affairs Australia, Melbourne, 1968

FUCHS, SIR VIVIAN & HILLARY, SIR EDMUND. *The Crossing of Antarctica: The Commonwealth Trans-Antarctic Expedition 1955-58*. Cassell, London, 1958

GORMLY, P. *ANARE First Aid Manual*. Third edition. Antarctic Division, Department of Science and Technology, Hobart, 1984

HOLLIN, J. & CAMERON, R. *I.G.Y. Glaciological Work at Wilkes Station, Antarctica*. Journal of Glaciology Vol. 3, No. 29, March 1961, The British Glaciological Society, Cambridge

HOSKING, E. & SAGE, B. *Antarctic Wildlife*. Croom Helm, London, 1982

HOWELL, M. & FORD, P. *Medical Mysteries*. Viking, Middlesex, England, 1985

JACKSON, A. (ed.). *ANARE Field Manual*. Second edition. Information Services Section, Antarctic Division, Department of Science and Technology, Hobart, 1982

JENKINS-SMITH, K. *Heard Island Odyssey*. HIDI·'Y' Enterprises, Norfolk Island, 1985

JOHNSON, P., BOND, C. & SIEGFRIED, R. *Antarctica: No Single Country — No Single Sea*. Hamlyn, London, 1979

JONGENS, S. 'Heard Island, Uphill' in *Aurora*, ANARE Club Journal, No.8, June 1983

LASERON, C. *South With Mawson: Reminiscences of the Australasian Antarctic Expedition, 1911-14*. Angus and Robertson, Sydney, 1957

LAW, P. *Antarctic Odyssey*. Heinemann, Melbourne, 1983

LAW, P. & BÉCHERVAISE, J. *ANARE: Australia's Antarctic Outposts*. Oxford University Press, Melbourne, 1957

LAURITZEN, J. *Nella Dan's* ship's log, 1984/85, September-December 1987

LEDINGHAM, R. (ed.). *ANARE Bunger Hills Preliminary Scientific and Field Operation Report, January-March 1986*. Antarctic Division internal report, Antarctic Division, Department of Science, Hobart, 1986

LOVERING, J. & PRESCOTT, J. *Last of Lands. . . Antarctica*. Melbourne University Press, Melbourne, 1979

McKINNON, G. *Gazetteer Of The Australian Antarctic Territory*. ANARE Interim Reports, Series A (II) Geography, Publication No.75, Antarctic Division, Department of External Affairs, Melbourne, 1965

MAWSON, SIR DOUGLAS. *Home Of The Blizzard*. Abridged popular edition. Hodder & Stoughton, London, 1930

MIGOT, A. *The Lonely South*. Hart Davis, London, 1956

NATIONAL PARKS AND WILDLIFE SERVICE. *Macquarie Island Nature Reserve: Visitor's Handbook*. National Parks and Wildlife Service, Tasmania, 1987

PARER, D. & PARER-COOK, E. *Douglas Mawson — The Survivor*. Alella Books and the Australian Broadcasting Corporation, Melbourne, 1983

READER'S DIGEST. *Antarctica: Great Stories from the Frozen Continent*. Reader's Digest, Sydney, 1985

SMITH, J. *Specks In The Southern Ocean*. The Department of Geography and Planning, University of New England, Armidale, 1986

STALLMAN, S. *Gazetteer of the Australian Antarctic Territory*. ANARE Research Notes 15, Antarctic Division, Department of Science and Technology, Hobart, 1983

TEMPLE, P. *The Sea And The Snow: The South Indian Ocean Expedition to Heard Island*. Cassell, Melbourne, 1966

THORNTON, M. (ed.). *Heard Island Expedition 1983*. Spirit of Adventure, Sydney, 1983

THWAITES, R. *1984 Operations Report*. Casey glaciology field program. Antarctic Division internal report, Antarctic Division, Department of Science, Hobart, January 1986

THWAITES, R. *Glaciological Measurements on the Southern Traverse Route from Casey Into Wilkes Land*. Draft report. Antarctic Division, Department of Science, Hobart, 1987

US NAVY HYDROGRAPHIC OFFICE. *A Functional Glossary of Ice Terminology*. US Navy Hydrographic Office, Washington, D.C., 1952

Glossary

Aeronomy The science of the study of the upper atmosphere. The building at Mawson in which most of the upper atmosphere physics experiments are conducted is called Aeronomy.

Anemometer An instrument for measuring wind speed.

Antarctic Division The Australian Commonwealth Government organisation, formed in 1948, which manages the Australian National Antarctic Research Expeditions, providing planning and logistics support.

AAE Australasian Antarctic Expedition, 1911-1914. This expedition was organised and led by Douglas Mawson (later Sir). Three bases were set up, one at Macquarie Island and two in Antarctica: at Commonwealth Bay and on the Shackleton Ice Shelf. Besides its prolific scientific results, the expedition was the first to use radio communication from Antarctica.

ANARE Australian National Antarctic Research Expeditions. This name, first given in 1947, refers to Australia's activities in the Antarctic and subantarctic regions.

AWS Automatic weather station. Designed by technical staff at Antarctic Division, the stations are erected in remote locations and provide measurements on temperature, wind speed and direction, atmospheric pressure and solar radiation via a satellite link.

ATK Aviation turbine kerosene. An aircraft fuel used in many of the diesel-powered vehicles on the Antarctic stations because of its low freezing point.

Donga A colloquial term referring to an expeditioner's bedroom at an Antarctic station.

Drift Airborne snow particles driven by the wind. Ground-drift blows low over the surface and does not obscure visibility.

Fast ice Floating ice which is attached to the shore or held in place by islands or grounded icebergs.

FIBEX First International BIOMASS Experiment. An experiment in 1980/81 in which twelve nations took part. Its main aim was to survey the distribution of krill in the Indian and South Atlantic sectors of the Southern Ocean.
BIOMASS: an acronym for Biological Investigations of Marine Antarctic Systems and Stocks. BIOMASS was an international program running from 1976 to 1986 to investigate the Antarctic marine ecosystem.

First-year ice Floating ice not more than one year old.

Hagglunds A tracked, amphibious vehicle manufactured by Hagglunds of Sweden.

Helideck A landing place for helicopters on a ship.

Hoarfrost Ice crystals formed on objects by condensation of water vapour from the air when the temperature is below freezing point. The crystals often have the shape of needles or scales.

Krill (Euphausia Superba) A shrimp-like crustacean up to six centimetres long which is abundant in Antarctic waters. It is an important food source for many larger animals, including whales, seals, penguins and other birds.

Lead A narrow but navigable passage in pack ice.

LARC Lighter: Amphibious Resupply Craft. An amphibious vehicle used to unload cargo and personnel from resupply ships. The LARCs are owned and crewed by the Australian Army.

Met An abbreviation for meteorological.

Moraine Rock debris carried and deposited by a glacier.

Pancake ice Pieces of new ice, roughly circular, about 0.3 to 3 metres across, having raised rims due to the cakes rotating and colliding with each other.

Parhelion A bright spot on, or just outside, a solar halo. A parhelion occurs on either side of the halo. The parhelia, also called mock suns or sundogs, are caused by reflection and refraction of light by ice crystals in the atmosphere.

Polynya (Plural: polynyi) Any sizeable area of water, other other than a lead, encompassed by pack ice or fast ice.

Radiosonde An instrument carried by a balloon which transmits temperature, pressure, and relative humidity to a receiver on the ground.

Sastrugi Irregular ridges of snow formed by windborne drift eroding the surface. The ridges run in the same direction as the prevailing wind.

Skidoo A motorised snow toboggan.

Slot The colloquial term for a crevasse.

Snowblindness Caused by ultraviolet light burning the cornea of the eye. The eyes become painful and watery and the patient finds light intolerable. Treatment involves bandaging the eyes closed to rest them. A lot of ultraviolet light is reflected off snow, but snowblindness can be prevented by wearing dark glasses.

Tide crack A crack around the shoreline separating ice attached to the shore (the icefoot) from the floating ice. The crack is formed by the tide raising and lowering the floating ice.

Traverse A journey over a significant distance (as opposed to a short field trip) and usually incorporating some kind of survey work.

Index

Text references are in ordinary type; illustration references are in italic.

On Christmas Eve 1987,
Nella Dan sank off Macquarie Island
in the Southern Ocean.
No lives were lost,
but she took with her over
twenty-six years of memories

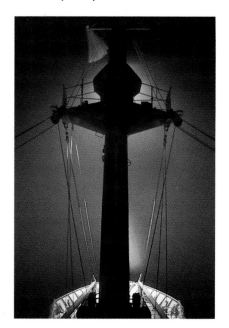